PROFICIENCY-
BASED ASSESSMENT

process, not product

troy   mark   anthony r.   eric

GOBBLE   **ONUSCHECK**   **REIBEL**   **TWADELL**

Solution Tree | Press
a division of
Solution Tree

555 North Morton Street
Bloomington, IN 47404
800.733.6786 (toll free) / 812.336.7700
FAX: 812.336.7790

email: info@solution-tree.com
solution-tree.com

Visit **go.solution-tree.com/assessment** to download the reproducibles in this book.

Printed in the United States of America

19   18   17   16   15   1   2   3   4   5

Library of Congress Cataloging-in-Publication Data

Gobble, Troy.

  Proficiency-based assessment : process, not product / by Troy Gobble, Mark Onuscheck, Anthony R. Reibel, and Eric Twadell.

       pages cm

  Includes bibliographical references and index.

  ISBN 978-1-936763-54-2 (perfect bound) 1. Educational tests and measurements--United States. 2. Academic achievement--Data processing. I. Title.

  LB3051.G54 2015

  371.26--dc23

                         2015027620

Solution Tree
Jeffrey C. Jones, CEO
Edmund M. Ackerman, President

Solution Tree Press
President: Douglas M. Rife
Associate Acquisitions Editor: Kari Gillesse
Editorial Director: Lesley Bolton
Managing Production Editor: Caroline Weiss
Production Editor: Tara Perkins
Proofreader: Elisabeth Abrams
Text and Cover Designer: Abigail Bowen

The authors intend to donate all of their royalties to the Stevenson High School Foundation.

To our spouses (Danielle, Juliet, Kathy, and Anne) and to our children (Owen, Claire, Adeline, Sofia, William, Tony, Andrew, Kaitlyn, and Lauren) for the immeasurable love and joy they bring to our lives each and every day.

Acknowledgments

Our understanding of proficiency-based assessment has been heavily influenced by the experts who have been helping schools shift from a culture of testing to a culture of assessment for more than twenty years. These experts include Dylan Wiliam, Paul Black, Rick Stiggins, Jan Chappuis, Robert Marzano, and Larry Ainsworth, just to name a few. Although we did not directly collaborate with these experts on this project, their ideas have influenced our own. We would also like to thank assessment expert Cassandra Erkens for bringing clarity to an important element in this work.

At our own school's dedication on September 7, 1965, the first superintendent, Harold Banser, said of Adlai E. Stevenson High School, "We are born out of conflict, nurtured by adversity, and destined for greatness." Whatever measure of greatness our school has achieved fifty years later is a direct result of the hard work, dedication, and commitment to continuous improvement of the board of education, administration, faculty, staff, and students of Stevenson High School. We consider it the blessing of a lifetime to work at Stevenson, and we are grateful for our colleagues' unrelenting pursuit of our school's mission of success for every student. We extend a special thank-you to Thomas Loew, who always helps his students achieve new levels, not only on the CPR exam but also in health and wellness.

Close readers of the Professional Learning Communities at Work™ literature might wonder why four leaders from Adlai E. Stevenson High School—widely considered the birthplace of the PLC movement—rarely mention PLCs in this text. The answer is quite simple. While our friend and former principal and superintendent Rick DuFour, architect of PLC at Work along with Rebecca DuFour and Robert Eaker, was leading Stevenson High School for more than twenty-five years, he was insistent that *professional learning community* is less of a noun and more of a verb. Becoming a PLC is a way of life—a culture of a district, school, or team—not a formal meeting once a week. We took it as a personal challenge to write a book describing a model PLC culture without relying on an acronym to serve as the authority for change and improvement. We are forever grateful for the work that Rick has done to help us to shape a PLC culture here at Stevenson High School and in schools around the world.

Finally, we are especially thankful for our friends at Solution Tree for sharing best practices in our profession and telling the stories of reform and continuous improvement in schools for many years. Thank you to Jeff Jones, Ed Ackerman, Douglas Rife, and the entire Solution Tree team who supported our efforts and pushed us to share our ideas in this book. And, enough cannot be said of our new friend and editor Tara Perkins, who has been patient, kind, and supportive as we have tried to merge four voices into one story of professional growth and development in proficiency-based assessment.

Solution Tree Press would like to thank the following reviewers:

Stafford D. Boyd
Director of Title Programs,
    Professional Development, and
    Secondary Teaching & Learning
Newberg Public Schools
Newberg, Oregon

Virgel Hammonds
Superintendent
RSU 2
Hallowell, Maine

Don Kordosky
Superintendent
Oakridge School District #76
Oakridge, Oregon

Greg Potter
Superintendent of Schools
Regional School Unit 19
Newport, Maine

Delphia Young
Executive Director of Research,
    Evaluation, Assessment, and
    Accountability
Clayton County Public Schools
Jonesboro, Georgia

Visit **go.solution-tree.com/assessment** to download the reproducibles in this book.

Table of Contents

About the Authors

Troy Gobble is the principal of Adlai E. Stevenson High School in Lincolnshire, Illinois. Troy joined Stevenson as assistant principal for teaching and learning for the 2010–11 school year. He served in a similar capacity at Riverside Brookfield High School in 2009–10, and spent a total of nine years at the school. Troy was chairman of the science department prior to becoming assistant principal and also taught physics. He began his teaching career at Carl Sandburg High School in 1992.

In 2006, Troy earned the Outstanding Illinois High School Physics Teacher Award from the Illinois section of the American Association of Physics Teachers.

Troy earned his bachelor of science degree in secondary science education from the University of Illinois at Urbana-Champaign. He has master's degrees from Eastern Illinois University (natural science-physics) and Benedictine University (educational administration), and is completing his doctorate in educational leadership through DePaul University.

To learn more about Troy's work, visit his website at www.troygobble.com.

Mark Onuscheck is director of curriculum, instruction, and assessment at Adlai E. Stevenson High School in Lincolnshire, Illinois. He is a former English teacher and director of communication arts. In his current role, Mark works with academic divisions around professional learning, articulation, curricular and instructional revision, evaluation, assessment, social and emotional learning, technologies, and implementation of the Common Core State Standards. He is also an adjunct professor at DePaul University.

Mark was awarded the Quality Matters Star Award for his work in online teaching. He helps build curriculum and instructional practices for TimeLine Theatre's arts integration program for Chicago Public Schools. Additionally, he is a grant recipient from the National Endowment for the Humanities and a member of the Association for Supervision and Curriculum Development, National Council of Teachers of English, International Literacy Association (formerly International Reading Association), and Learning Forward.

Mark earned a bachelor's degree in English and classical studies from Allegheny College and a master's degree in teaching from the University of Pittsburgh.

Anthony R. Reibel is director of assessment, research, and evaluation at Adlai E. Stevenson High School in Lincolnshire, Illinois. He administers assessments, manages student achievement data, and oversees instructional practice. Anthony began his professional career as a technology specialist and entrepreneur. After managing several businesses, he became a Spanish teacher at Stevenson. He has also served as a curricular team leader, core team leader, coach, and club sponsor.

In 2010, Anthony received recognition from the state of Illinois, and the Illinois Computing Educators named him Technology Educator of the Year. He is a member of the Association for Supervision and Curriculum Development, Illinois Principals Association, Illinois Computing Educators, and American Council on the Teaching of Foreign Languages.

He earned a bachelor's degree in Spanish from Indiana University and master's degrees (one in curriculum and instruction and a second in educational leadership) from Roosevelt University.

To learn more about Anthony's work, follow him on Twitter @areibel.

Eric Twadell, PhD, is superintendent of Adlai E. Stevenson High School in Lincolnshire, Illinois. He has been a social studies teacher, curriculum director, and assistant superintendent for leadership and organizational development.

Stevenson High School has been described by the United States Department of Education (USDE) as "the most recognized and celebrated school in America" and is one of only three schools to win the USDE National Blue Ribbon Schools award on four occasions. Stevenson was one of the first comprehensive schools designated a New American High School by USDE as a model of successful school reform and is repeatedly cited as one of the top high schools in the United States and the birthplace of the Professional Learning Communities at Work™ process.

Eric is a coauthor who has also written several professional articles. As a dedicated PLC practitioner, he has worked with state departments of education and local schools and districts throughout the United States to achieve school improvement and reform. An accessible and articulate authority on PLC concepts, Eric brings hands-on experience to his presentations and workshops.

In addition to his teaching and leadership roles, he has been involved in coaching numerous athletic teams and facilitating outdoor education and adventure travel programs. He is a member of many professional organizations.

He earned a master's degree in curriculum and instruction and a doctorate in educational leadership and policy studies from Loyola University Chicago.

To book Troy Gobble, Mark Onuscheck, Anthony R. Reibel, or Eric Twadell for professional development, contact pd@solution-tree.com.

Introduction

We are believers. We do not need to be at all convinced that powerful formative assessment experiences have the potential to transform teaching and learning as we know it. The experts have weighed in time and time again:

> There is strong and rigorous evidence that improving formative assessment can raise standards and pupil's performance. There have been few initiatives in education with such a strong body of evidence to support a claim to raise standards. (Black & Wiliam, 1998, p. 20)

> Research on the effects of classroom assessment indicate that it might be one of the most powerful weapons in a teacher's arsenal. An effective standards-based, formative assessment program can help to dramatically enhance student achievement throughout the K–12 system. (Marzano, 2006, p. 2, back cover)

> Formative assessment is a potentially transformative instructional tool that, if clearly understood and adroitly employed, can benefit both educators and their students. . . . Formative assessment constitutes the key cornerstone of clearheaded instructional thinking. Formative assessment represents evidence-based instructional decision-making. If you want to become more instructionally effective, and if you want your students to achieve more, then formative assessments should be for you. (Popham, 2008, pp. 3, 15)

We have not only learned from experts about how to develop and implement powerful new assessment strategies but we have seen it happen in our own school; likewise, we have seen it happen in classrooms across North America that are on the cutting edge of assessment reform.

The great hope of assessment reform has focused our attention on the role of formative assessment experiences, where teachers generate meaningful feedback about student learning that allows for appropriate differentiation and adjustments to instruction. Moreover, teachers provide students with clear data and evidence related to students' strengths and areas for improvement that are tied to specific courses' objectives and outcomes.

While we are absolutely convinced that rethinking and redesigning assessment experiences are essential to improving student learning and achievement, our fear is that there is a growing number of educators who have developed an irrational exuberance for testing, analytics, and big data that will leave the promise of worthwhile assessment reform unfulfilled.

We have found that in many cases the traditional gaps that have existed between curriculum, instruction, and assessment have not been filled in. While educators have been called on to develop new and improved assessment experiences for students, we have seen that while many may be literate in the distinction between formative and summative assessments, there is an equal number of our colleagues who are unsure and unable to actually develop, implement, and evaluate truly formative assessment experiences for students.

A Lack of Clarity

We believe that successful formative assessment initiative implementation requires a synchronized overhaul of curriculum development, instructional implementation, and assessment practices. In many schools and classrooms, we have seen a lack of clarity regarding formative assessment and the need for the changes in our approach to curriculum development and instructional delivery. Ultimately, this lack of clarity causes teachers to continuously and unknowingly keep curriculum, instruction, and assessment separated from one another. When curriculum, instruction, and assessment are not understood as one seamless, integrated approach to teaching and learning, formative assessment becomes especially difficult to institutionalize. Building clarity is paramount to leading successful change initiatives. In fact, our experience has revealed that in districts, schools, and classrooms where formative assessment has become summative, there is specifically a lack of clarity regarding the *why*, the *how*, and the *what* of formative assessment.

The Why of Formative Assessment

In *Start With Why*, Simon Sinek (2009) makes a strong case for leading innovation and change out of what he calls *The Golden Circle*. The Golden Circle articulates an understanding of leading change that is simple and calls leaders and followers to answer the *why* question of change before diving into the questions and answers related to the *how* and *what* questions. In many schools, educators have come to regard formative assessment as just one more thing they have to do before and after their instruction. Without a clear *why*, there exists no instructional purpose for formative assessment, leaving many of us to assume that teachers use formative assessments only to determine the effectiveness of their instruction and so students can monitor their learning. This limited perspective, caused by a lack of coherence and clarity, causes formative assessment to become narrowly focused, and leaves some of us to view it as a mechanism to verify learning.

The *why* of formative assessment must not be misunderstood—formative assessment is *not* intended to be verification or confirmation of learning. Formative assessment, when done well, is a flexible instructional practice that perpetually and strategically changes based on students' academic needs and output.

The How of Formative Assessment

As we work with teachers across North America, and even within our own school, we sometimes see a tendency toward a narrowly focused understanding of how to develop and implement formative assessment practices. When we lack clarity of the *how* of formative assessment, we often see assessment as a series of events with limited variation of assessment tools. We believe that good, high-quality assessment is a process—a process that takes developed techniques and awareness to master. To help discover these techniques (the *how* of formative assessment) we as educators must resist the temptation to define it too narrowly. Formative assessment must remain a flexible and dynamic process that is not limited to a specific label and form. With so many of us trying to define and clarify what good assessment should look like, it is no wonder that a constant question from teachers remains, "Yeah, but *how* do I do formative assessment?"

As you will see throughout this book, we believe that the *how* of successful formative assessment is achieved by first and foremost developing consensus around proficiency and then articulating and employing instructional practices that support students developing understanding and skills through the intentional manipulation of student evidence and reflection to generate a desired proficiency.

The What of Formative Assessment

When most educators are asked to define formative assessment and state its purpose, they respond with statements such as the following.

- "Formative assessment is an opportunity to check in and see how my students are doing."

- "Formative assessment gives me a picture of how well I taught the curriculum."

- "Formative assessment provides me with data on my instruction."

- "Formative assessment helps me determine student growth."

Their answers have a clear pattern. In general, most teachers, parents, and students see the *what* of formative assessment as a result that is inserted into a time line of instruction to check for student understanding and verify achievement—something separate and distinct from the instructional process. When this happens, formative assessment risks being viewed as an isolated event and a product that ultimately muddles the assessment process and clouds its ideal purpose.

As a result of the lack of clarity regarding what good, quality formative assessment is and looks like in practice, teachers and leaders spend countless hours asking if the formative assessments that have been deployed have been effective. Ultimately, when formative assessment is implemented poorly, the experience drags us toward conversations of accomplishment and pulls us away from the real dialogue of assessment, which requires a new strategy.

A New Strategy

As practicing educators, we have spent considerable time and effort examining and experimenting with assessment methods—specifically formative assessment practices. Many of the current practices of formative assessment actually reflect traditional testing and summative assessment practices that are focusing educators who have the right intentions on the wrong work. As a result, we believe we need a new language and a new vocabulary regarding assessment—the simple formative versus summative dichotomy is not enough to help teachers understand the important difference that high-leverage assessment practices can have on student learning and achievement. Based on our experiences and our efforts to implement meaningful change in the areas of curriculum, instruction, and assessment, our hope is to support the development of new understandings of how assessment can improve the teaching and learning process. This new understanding and these new approaches must be focused on the concept of *proficiency*.

We have found that when we focus on developing teachers' and students' understanding of proficiency, meaningful assessment practices emerge that are truly incorporated into the instructional experience. Students develop an empowered awareness of how to *access* and *assess* their own thinking. Learning begins to grow; it becomes individualized, reflective, and self-driven. This new understanding and approach focus the curriculum, instruction, and assessment on the right questions and, when implemented correctly, combine these three elements into one, closing the gaps that often exist among them in traditional school settings. We refer to this practice as *proficiency-based assessment.*

Five Phases of Implementing Proficiency-Based Assessment

The work of developing proficiency-based assessment practices should not be done alone. Our best chance for making lasting and significant change comes through work done in collaboration. Likewise, change does not come easily through a "sit and get" stand-alone professional development day, nor through a "one-size-fits-all" model. Instead, high-quality professional development must recognize that individual teachers and collaborative teams vary in expertise, knowledge, and skill. We believe every teacher brings strengths and different capabilities to every conversation, and these multiple viewpoints must be valued and considered during the decision-making process for students. For this reason, we must differentiate professional learning with more focused, worthwhile experiences for our teachers. To do this, we must go back to some basics.

To create individualized, quality, and effective professional learning experiences, we rely on the long-standing research grounded in the creative process. Psychologist and author Mihaly Csikszentmihalyi (1990) presents this process in five interconnected and overlapping phases, as follows.

1. **Preparation** is becoming immersed in problematic issues that are interesting and arouse curiosity. *Preparation* is the term that psychologists apply to the first stage of the creative process, when individuals are starting out and struggling to perfect their craft. Inspiration is what drives the curiosity of both great artists and scientists to persevere through their years of hard work.

2. **Incubation** refers to the period during which ideas churn around below the threshold of consciousness. After an individual has started working on a solution to a problem or has had an idea leading to a novel approach to an effort, the individual enters the incubation stage. According to research psychologists, this stage can last hours, days, months, or years. When individuals try to solve problems consciously, it becomes a linear process, but when problems are left to incubate or simmer, unexpected combinations occur. These unexpected combinations form domain-changing breakthroughs.

3. **Insight** is the aha! moment when the puzzle starts to come together. The insight stage is also called the *eureka experience*. Some psychologists call it *illumination*. It's the exact moment in time when a problem that an individual has been trying to solve—for days, months, or years—comes together in his or her mind to form a clear resolution. This resolution only emerges after a complex and lengthy process.

4. **Evaluation** occurs when deciding if the insight is valuable and worth pursuing. During the final stage of the creative process, individuals must decide if their insights are novel and make sense. In other words, they must analyze the insights to determine if they're truly worth pursuing. If the insight continues to excite and motivate the individual to go forward, then the hard work of turning the creation into a reality begins. Some creativity researchers, such as Harvard University's Teresa M. Amabile (1983), cite motivation as the key factor in the creative process. Regardless of the ingenuity, novelty, or originality of an idea, artwork, or scientific invention, if the creator is unmotivated, the work will never become a reality.

5. **Elaboration** involves translating the insight into a final work and constantly nuancing or revising. Throughout the creativity literature, many who have created products that literally changed their domains or disciplines state the necessity of hard work and revision. Yet at the same time, they also state that it doesn't seem like work at all but seems more like play. It's the process of creating that drives individuals forward toward continuous growth and improvement.

These five phases of the creative process model the way we want to nurture professional *growth* and *positive changes* by seeking the expertise, collaboration, and inquiry of educators. Yes, making changes with other experts is demanding, but the rewards for teaching and learning are both exciting and extraordinarily valuable for professional learning. They take hold because educators spend time collaborating and consulting with one another each step of the way. The change not only sustains, it evolves to get better. As the education profession seeks to address its many different and complex challenges, the creative process reminds us to be prepared for change, to incubate change and not rush to decisions, to generate insights into change, to thoughtfully evaluate changes that are made, and to continuously improve and evolve.

By building professional learning around these five phases, we see greater progress because we are supporting teachers as they interact differently within each of the five phases of creating change. By focusing in on these five phases, our teachers and teams get better professional development that (1) supports learning and the role of questioning, (2) recognizes the value and the inevitability of pushback, (3) provides specific environments that open up thinking and our teacher's creative aha! moments, (4) allows reflective professional development that addresses evaluation and discernment, and (5) develops a culture of continuous improvement and thoughtful revision.

As you read, consider why each phase is important to developing long-lasting, sustained commitments to build a stronger school supported through the efforts of all team members. More specifically, as you read, we hope to provide you a pathway to implement proficiency-based assessment—a change we think is a significant one schools should be making as we all work to address student growth and learning.

Structure of This Book

In chapter 1, we will (1) establish a foundational understanding of proficiency-based assessment and the mindset that must accompany this educational change, (2) identify the greater value of proficiency-based assessment for teaching and learning, and (3) synthesize what we've learned about implementing proficiency-based assessment through the many collaborative conversations we've led in our school as we have worked as a professional learning community. Chapters 2 through 6 will address and illustrate how teams can approach a shift toward proficiency-based assessment in their classrooms using the five phases of the creative process.

Each chapter dedicates itself to explaining each phase more fully, demonstrates change through the eyes of our teachers, and identifies key strategies to support a change to proficiency-based assessment. As you'll see, each phase fosters powerful, smarter discussions around teaching and student learning.

As this book unfolds in chapters 2 through 6, we outline one curriculum team's journey to implement proficiency-based assessment, and we illustrate how these five phases of the creative process are used to integrate proficiency-based assessment into collaborative work. The team's school and members are fictional but were developed with some of the best teachers we know in mind. The members of our team will navigate the challenges, pitfalls, and successes as they engage in each stage of the professional learning process. Along the way they collaborate, debate ideas, and work to build consensus as they reach toward a new approach to assessment that is grounded in better teaching and learning practices. While the resources the team consults and quotes in are also fictional, they are representative of the extant literature many collaborative teams are working with regarding discussions of proficiency-based assessment.

While we present each of these phases in order in chapters 2 through 6, it's important to note that this is only a way of separating phases that build toward a progressive understanding. In the end, and as you will see, phases are recursive and often overlapping. Also, it's important to understand that no one phase is better than another phase. Professionals always have insights and go back and prepare, think, or evaluate. This process is not meant to be linear or formulaic. Each and every phase is equally important and equally demanding. Individual educators and teams of educators will move in and among these phases of the creative process—they will revisit them, questioning, reacting to, thinking about, and returning to them at different times. That is a good thing, allowing professionals to reflect, learn, develop new ideas, and build on those ideas.

The team will first move through the preparation stage in chapter 2, where quality assessment principles are brought to life through the introduction and negotiation of new vocabulary, solidifying a foundational knowledge of how curriculum, instruction, and assessment interact. During this stage, the team's feedback structures are questioned, and the team members begin to see the value of student reflection as a powerful learning experience. In this stage, we will see the team learn about new norms of assessment and instruction, they will become more informed about the *why* behind proficiency-based assessment, and they will create a shared understanding of proficiency-based assessment.

In chapters 3 and 4, our team will enter the thinking phases of development: the incubation and insight stages. Here, the team wrestles with new concepts, such as proficiency, scaled targets, and common formative assessment. We will observe the team struggling with the tension between the traditional practice of grading and reporting and grappling with new ideas related to standards-based reporting and proficiency-based targets. Here teams confront long-standing traditions and practices, and they think more specifically about the 21st century learner, what quality instruction needs to be, what effective targets identify the learning for all students, and what it means to implement better assessment practices.

In chapter 5, we will see the team emerge in the evaluation phase. During this phase, the team works to create a reflective environment around formative assessment and their new insights. Through experimentation with this new mindset around proficiency-based targets, common formative assessments, and different grading and reporting structures, we see our team reflect on the appropriateness and effectiveness of these new collaborative learning environments. By the end of this journey, we will see the team take responsibility for further revision and continuous improvement. Through each phase, you will notice the team members reflecting on teaching and learning, coming to view the assessment process as more of a catalyst for the learning rather than as a mechanism for testing, and they will begin to create classrooms where all students can reach proficiency in a rigorous curriculum.

Finally, in chapter 6, the team members will arrive at the elaboration stage with a clear connectedness between their work and a newfound purpose and commitment to student learning. With fully developed examples of proficiency-based assessment, the members of the team will work to deploy evidence-based grading practices. Furthermore, you will see them place more emphasis on effective feedback structures in their classroom and practice instruction that creates a perpetually dynamic learning process. The team's elaboration capacity with proficiency-based assessment becomes evident through more accurate reflection practices, revisions to instruction, implementation of evidence-driven grading, and assessment that is in line with instruction. Ultimately, we see the team's patterns of teaching merge to unify their shared curriculum, instruction, and assessment into a singular process with a mindset of continuous improvement.

The use of these phases as a professional development model within schools helps initiate and sustain a culture of innovation and continuous improvement—an engaging world where curriculum, instruction, and assessment work together as one. We are confident that by working with this framework and implementing these principles you will create a high-yield environment that will have lasting effects on students, teaching, and learning and the culture of your school.

Chapter 1

Beyond the Formative and Summative Divide

Providing formative assessment experiences for students is a growing practice that has many positive effects. Many teachers have been doing a wonderful job of learning formative assessment practices that have the intended benefit of providing teachers with information to adjust their instruction, and providing students with feedback on their learning so they can address their own learning gaps.

Throughout this book, we will uphold the vision of the formative assessment experts; however, we will challenge the way in which many of the formative assessment practices are actually implemented. Our intention is to introduce a new assessment model that successfully promotes healthy formative assessment practices that are *not* summative and a curriculum, instruction, and assessment structure that is flexible, progressive, and dynamic.

This book is designed to provide clarity regarding proficiency-based assessment and a professional development model to implement it with fidelity. In this chapter, we frame a summary of important elements of proficiency-based assessment and its relationship to teaching and learning, offering a synthesis to ensure communication is clear, consistent, and coherent. We hope this chapter will help *support* teachers and teacher leaders in learning, understanding, and implementing proficiency-based assessment. As the book progresses, we hope our work can also help institutionalize proficiency-based assessment in a way that builds on the good assessment work teachers, curriculum teams, and schools are already doing.

Recognizing the Need for Proficiency-Based Assessment

As we have worked within our own school and with teachers around North America, we have witnessed firsthand the important and significant changes that our profession is making with respect to testing and assessment. We are especially excited about the focus we see on developing more formative assessment experiences for students. At the same time, however, we have noticed that the conversation around formative and summative assessment is often reduced to generalities and catchphrases—"The difference between formative and summative is a lot like the difference between a CAT scan and an autopsy" or "The difference between a formative and summative assessment is in how the assessment gets used." As we developed a commitment to formative assessment in our own school, we realized that if we hope to make significant and lasting change to current practices, we also need to change the conversation around assessment practices and teaching and learning. For assessment to drive instructional improvement and student learning in ways in which we hoped, we knew that we would need to move beyond the simple dichotomy of assessments as being either formative or summative.

Each and every day, educators are working tirelessly to move students through a guaranteed and viable curriculum (Marzano, 2003). However, the further we travel on this journey, we find ourselves lost in a labyrinth of new and different essential standards, objectives, and targets. If we are not careful, we can become easily confused by all of the jargon and terminology, and we can spend a lot of valuable time making wrong turns while spending countless hours developing curriculum frameworks, unit plans, and pacing guides.

Most schools and classrooms follow a fairly traditional curriculum, instruction, and assessment cycle. At some point near the start of the school year, teachers map the curriculum plan, and unit plans are developed and agreed on. Throughout the year, teachers implement instructional activities tied to the curriculum, and periodically, they assess students' progress toward the curriculum standards and objectives. This traditional pattern of curriculum design, illustrated in figure 1.1, is often understood and implemented in a linear progression.

Develop Curriculum → Provide Instruction → Implement Assessment

---

Figure 1.1: Traditional pacing layout for teaching.

We often hear teachers describe how in their experiences these three domains of their work are often applied as separate activities that don't necessarily work in concert with one another. This is certainly not new—historical practice and an ingrained way of thinking about curriculum, instruction, and assessment have, in many ways, married us to a view that teaching and learning is a series of separate elements, laid out on a linear time line.

To combat this traditional approach to curriculum, instruction, and assessment, many new ideas about instruction and assessment methods have emerged. Specifically, following the publication of the article "Inside the Black Box" (Black & Wiliam, 1998), formative assessment has become an accepted and essential tool in a teacher's toolbox. While the benefits of formative assessment are many, we are finding that, more often than not, formative assessment is being interpreted as a separate and distinct experience from instruction that has the effect of perpetuating and simply extending the old linear progression of curriculum, instruction, and assessment, as seen in figure 1.2.

Develop Curriculum → Provide Instruction → Implement Formative Assessment → Provide Adjusted Instruction → Implement Summative Assessment

Figure 1.2: Traditional pacing layout for formative assessment implementation.

While this linear approach may feel natural and comfortable for some teachers, it creates learning gaps that both teachers and students can fall into. As it is difficult to do two things at once, teachers are often forced to choose between developing curriculum, providing instruction, implementing formative assessment, providing adjusted instruction, and implementing summative assessments. This forced choice causes formative assessment practices to go underutilized, be inappropriately applied, or both. The lines between formative and summative become blurred, and we find ourselves right back in a linear instructional model.

In some classrooms, teachers implement and students experience formative assessments in a manner that is similar to summative assessments. When this happens, teachers and students fall into teaching and learning gaps that force assessment to be thought of as a systematic verification or substantiation of learning. Therefore, assessment becomes a time-out from learning in order to verify learning. In this way, assessment pauses the learning process to see if learning has occurred or to prove learning has occurred.

While intending to provide formative feedback, teachers are often implementing formative assessment on the linear time line (figure 1.2). When teachers are *implementing* formative assessment, they are not really *facilitating* formative assessment experiences for students. When assessment becomes an *event*—something altogether different from students' instructional experience and the teacher's learning intentions—we have lost the power of authentic and powerful formative assessment. Meaningful assessment experiences should be seamless and fully ingrained into instruction and students' learning experiences. Ideally, for the student, there would be no distinction; there would be no gap between the instructional and assessment experiences.

To achieve this ideal, assessment must be considered an instructional practice. As we discuss throughout this book, assessment, when done well, provides a unique and compelling portal through which to interact with students and their learning. We maintain that assessment is the *only* component in our teaching and learning practice that can simultaneously measure the rigor of the curriculum, prove the validity and effectiveness of instructional practice, promote authentic reflection, and calibrate and interpret student performance, learning, and achievement.

Understanding the Role of Proficiency

In the proficiency-based assessment model, we define proficiency as an intended state of competency that serves as a learning outcome. Since proficiency acts as *the* learning outcome and not as a *means to achieve* a learning outcome, a powerful balance among curriculum, instruction, and assessment can be realized. Identifying proficiency at the center of curriculum, instruction, and assessment has not been the traditional starting point for conversations among teachers when we dive into our curriculum work. In our experience, however, we have found great success when we are willing to rethink our traditional assumptions and we move proficiency-based assessment to the focus of our collaborative conversations and our teaching and learning practice. Utilizing proficiency-based assessment strategies supports teachers' efforts to bring harmony and congruence to their work on curriculum, instruction, and assessment, and, most importantly, students experience the following benefits.

1. Students learn new strategies to reflect on their thinking and learning.

2. Students are more able to internalize feedback from others.

3. Students develop strategies to provide feedback on their own learning.

4. Students develop a more flexible knowledge around content and skills.

Proficiency-based assessment then becomes the process of creating, supporting, and monitoring student reflection and thought patterns to achieve an intended state of competency. It also allows us to assess whether the student is able to demonstrate proficiencies outlined in the curriculum and whether our instruction is facilitating learning.

While we acknowledge and believe wholeheartedly in the work of formative assessment experts, we would humbly suggest that when we do not keep a thorough understanding of proficiency at the heart of the instructional process, assessment risks becoming nothing more than an isolated snapshot in time—disconnected from intended curriculum intentions and instructional experiences.

Incorporating the Elements of Proficiency-Based Assessment

There are three elements of proficiency-based assessment that not only support quality instruction and curriculum but also, more importantly, create powerful assessments that align with a proficiency expectation. These elements of proficiency-based assessment are as follows.

1. Proficiency-based targets
2. Proficiency-based instruction
3. Proficiency-based reflection

Incorporating these elements of proficiency-based assessment in the design phase of curriculum, instruction, and assessment helps frame clear and manageable pathways to supporting student learning. In addition, proficiency-based assessment creates a wonderfully powerful framework that helps students detect patterns of competence in their own work. Students begin to develop a heightened awareness of their own ability, cultivate healthy perspectives of their own growth opportunities and potential, and learn how to meaningfully reflect on their learning. Simply put, proficiency-based assessment ensures that students constantly maintain a relationship with the teacher's expectation of proficiency.

Element 1: Proficiency-Based Targets

Although there is a mountain of literature on how to develop student learning targets, writing high-quality targets remains an elusive practice for many educators. While there may be lots of reasons why this is true, we have personally found that some of our colleagues were not entirely clear on the differences among standards, objectives, and targets, their purpose, and the role of learning targets in the instructional and assessment process. We believe that the absence of well-designed and healthy student-learning targets is one of the reasons we see gaps among curriculum, instruction, and assessment in teachers' collaborative work and in teaching and learning experiences with students.

So what makes a target healthy and effective? As we have developed our understanding of proficiency-based assessment, we have found that the health and effectiveness of a learning target depends on the following essential components.

- Targets must be based on proficiency.
- Targets must be measurable.
- Targets must represent a gradation of learning.

When learning targets are proficiency based, measurable, and represent a gradation of learning, they become powerful tools to clearly communicate our learning expectations and they are more effective in guiding teaching and learning.

Targets Must Be Based on Proficiency

While we are excited that many conversations in assessment circles have focused on the importance of learning targets, we are surprised that there doesn't seem to be consensus from the experts on what exactly a learning target is and its purpose. Teachers believe a learning target is a specific understanding, skill, or product that a student must produce or demonstrate. And so, when working with learning targets, many teachers ask themselves if the target is *specific* enough for students. However, specificity in and of itself is an inadequate measure of the health of a student learning target.

In *Learning Targets*, assessment experts Connie Moss and Susan Brookhart (2012) state that learning targets express to students "the content and performance they are aiming for" (pp. 28–29). Of all of the definitions of learning targets we have heard over the years, we believe that Moss and Brookhart have helped push our thinking the furthest. Our view is that teachers have traditionally focused more on the content portion of the learning-target puzzle and less on the performance piece. It follows that proficiency must become the heart of a healthy learning target. Without a proficiency expectation, learning targets have the potential to remain isolated bits and pieces of content or skills that students are expected to master rather than tools to support student reflection and learning experiences.

To determine if a learning target is based on proficiency (rather than specificity), we have identified questions students should be able to answer if they are working with a well-developed, scaled proficiency-based target.

- How will I demonstrate this knowledge or skill?
- Why do I need to have this knowledge or perform this skill?
- How well do I need to perform this target?

If we are developing learning targets that contain the answers to these questions, we provide students with a clear picture of what we expect them to know and be able to do and more importantly, the level of understanding they need to demonstrate their proficiency. In other words, learning targets must contain the language of a clear proficiency expectation. For example, consider the target *Students will be able to explain the causes of World War I.*

Many teachers we work with would suggest that this is a clear, specific, and attainable target. However, if we look closely, we can see that this target does not contain any language that speaks to proficiency. Using the lens of proficiency-based assessment, teachers and students would be better served by presenting the target as *Students will be able to effectively explain the main political, economic, and social causes of World War I.*

With this simple addition of *effectively* and *main political, economic,* and *social,* the students now have a clearer picture of the competency that must be in the proposed skill, concept, or performance. At this point, a thoughtful reader may ask, "Is this really that much more specific? What does *effectively* really mean anyway? How does it speak to proficiency?"

Words like *effectively* may not seem to speak to a proficiency expectation. Simply adding and substituting a word like *effectively* is not enough. Teams must communicate to students how these proficiency words are connected to the supporting content or prerequisite skills that are needed to successfully satisfy the proficiency-based learning target. But before teachers and curriculum teams can do that, they must collaboratively agree on what a proficiency word such as *effectively* means. This can be accomplished in three ways.

1. Teachers and curriculum teams must develop clear *rubrics* that define the proficiency language and outline quality criteria that clarify proficiency language.

2. Teachers and curriculum teams must agree on what *instructional events* will promote and support the knowledge and skills outlined by the proficiency language.

3. Teachers and curriculum teams must engage in collaborative conversations about what the proficiency language might look like in student work.

Even after all of this work with a single word, our targets are still not complete. To create healthy proficiency-based targets, we must also make the targets measurable.

Targets Must Be Measurable

Measurable targets contain comparative and flexible language that clearly defines an expected state of proficiency. Without this measurability language, it is difficult for students to see a learning finish line beyond that of representation and reproduction. Learning targets must be written so that students can see and determine the proficiency expectation. For example, consider again the sample target we provided previously: *Students will be able to effectively explain the main political, economic, and social causes of World War I.* When we showed this revised target to some of our teachers, there were many positive responses to the addition of a proficiency expectation and the quality of the target. However, while the target may now contain proficiency language, it is not at all measurable.

If the same target *were* based on proficiency *and measurable*, it might look like this: *Using examples from class, students will be able to effectively explain the main political, economic, and social causes of World War I in a written analysis.*

By adding *Using examples from class* and *in a written analysis*, we move closer to a more focused expectation that begins to draw students' learning toward proficiency. Creating measurable learning targets allows for a healthy foundation for proficiency-based assessment, clear and purposeful instruction, and accurate and meaningful reflection on the part of students. When we get clear about proficiency, we help support students' understanding of the learning intention and expectation *and* state how well we expect students to know the content or skill. Still, we cannot stop target development here. If a learning target is going to be fully effective it must also represent a gradation of learning.

Targets Must Represent a Gradation of Learning

For most of us, when we think of targets, we see a series of concentric circles with a bull's-eye in the middle. We believe it is important that we see student learning targets in the same way. The center of these targets must be a clear articulation of proficiency for students that radiates outward. In other words, targets must represent a gradation of learning, not a list of content or skills to be learned. Connie Moss and Susan Brookhart (2012) refer to this gradation as a *learning trajectory*, and Robert Marzano (2009) identifies the same concept as a *learning progression*. This gradation of learning must be clearly laid out, understandable, and reachable for students.

When we consider targets and the rings that make up a target, one important fact should be made clear: not every student will be immediately proficient. Student understanding may be completely off base, hitting on an outer ring, or close to the center without quite being there. Teachers must begin to develop a learning trajectory for students that will help support their movement closer to the bull's-eye (proficiency). In many instances, targets have been written and taught less like a target and more like a light switch—it's on or off, and either students know it, or they don't. In proficiency-based assessment, targets must reflect multiple levels (gradations) of proficiency and create reflective learning opportunities for students to experience as they adapt their understanding and skills toward becoming proficient.

While we recognize and appreciate that this is not an entirely new concept, we believe that the ways in which we have traditionally attempted to scale targets have focused less on articulating gradations of learning and proficiency and more on levels of knowledge or task performance. For example, consider the following rubric from a high school U.S. history teacher's unit on World War I.

4—Compare and contrast the main causes of World War I.

3—Define main causes of World War I and their social implications.

2—Recognize key terms and figures from World War I.

1—List key terms and figures from World War I.

While these learning intentions reflect scaffolded knowledge and skills that students must know and be able to do as they move from simple to complex understanding, they do not provide students with clarity regarding the *gradation of learning* for a singular proficiency expectation. In other words, these targets might help students develop capacity in different tasks or skills, such as listing, recognizing, and so on, but they do not help students develop clarity regarding the levels of learning for a specific competency. In fact, if we were to look closely at the rubric, we would see that instead of one target that is clearly articulated and scaled to proficiency, actually we have four targets that each address a different skill that has no central proficiency expectation.

By creating a proficiency-based target that focuses in on *one* proficiency standard for one student learning target, we move toward a more solid foundation in which students will be able to transfer knowledge and skills between gradations of proficiency, develop new understanding of what proficiency is, and quickly identify when they are or are not proficient.

If we develop a gradation of learning and proficiency for our World War I target, it may look something like the following.

4—Using unique examples and opinions, students will be able to effectively explain the main political, economic, and social causes of World War I in a written analysis.

3—Using examples from class, students will be able to effectively explain the main political, economic, and social causes of World War I in a written analysis.

2—Using given definitions and terms, students will be able to effectively explain the main political, economic, and social causes of World War I in a written analysis.

1—Using a text, students will be able to effectively explain the main political, economic, and social causes of World War I in a written analysis.

By creating targets in this manner, students can now distinctly identify the once imperceptible differences between their current proficiency and the proficiency the teacher expects. Students need a clear learning destination; otherwise, they simply cannot identify their relative position to a teacher's expectation. When this happens, instruction simply loses the ability to move learning forward.

When targets contain proficiency and measurability and reflect a gradation of learning, they become extremely powerful and dynamic instructional tools. Proficiency-based targets are the essential elements in clear communication of learning expectations and proficiency-based assessment.

Element 2: Proficiency-Based Instruction

The second element of proficiency-based assessment is proficiency-based instruction. Simply put, we define proficiency-based instruction as deploying strategies and resources to respond to and reinforce students' reflective process. While we fully appreciate that this definition is not too dissimilar from the idea of differentiation, we believe that too many teachers engage in differentiating lessons without a clear sense of proficiency expectations defined and communicated to students. We often hear educators mistakenly describe differentiation as lecture on Monday, cooperative learning on Tuesday, video on Wednesday, lab work on Thursday, and review on Friday. However, this is simply a set of different modalities on different days of the week. Differentiation must go beyond content choices, processes, and student products and focus on helping individual students master proficiency expectations.

Without thoughtful identification and incorporation of proficiency levels into practice, traditional instruction often turns into a series of activities in search of a purpose. The lessons may appear neat, tidy, well developed, and competently implemented; however, they may not do anything to drive learning forward for individual students. In proficiency-based instruction, lessons are not sorted into a linear time line throughout a unit of study that is capped off by a summative test. We encourage teachers to consider that effective differentiation of instruction must include a multitude of learning pathways sewn together by a predetermined proficiency expectation of the student learning target. When done well, proficiency-based instruction involves the interplay of three intersecting components.

1. Planning to ensure that students meet a proficiency expectation
2. Focusing all resources on a proficiency expectation
3. Creating learning events that support a proficiency expectation

In classrooms that are focused on proficiency, we facilitate a learning environment for students that is highly responsive and dynamic, and we give students multiple opportunities to reflect on their own learning in relation to a crystal clear and understandable proficiency expectation. We remember one student in our school describing her experience with a teacher focusing on proficiency-based instruction: "In her class, you are not asked to just internalize facts and skills, you are figuring out how to organize and use your *own* thoughts to learn."

Planning to Ensure That Students Meet a Proficiency Expectation

Quality instruction begins with quality planning. Traditionally, most planning in most schools is done in light of the textbook, the pacing guide, or last year's lessons—in fact, for a long time, standard-issue equipment for new teachers was a desk, a bookcase, and a filing cabinet. Why a filing cabinet? To store lesson plans to be used again next year! The problem, of course, is that last year's lessons may not be appropriate for this year's students. Instead, we would like to see instructional planning begin with a proficiency-based and measurable learning target and a solid understanding of the gradations of learning that students must move through on their way toward proficiency.

Without proficiency-based learning targets placed at the center of planning, teachers may end up with one or more of the following types of lessons.

- **Engagement-focused lessons:** The focus of these lessons is on interactivity, such as group or partner activity with the content. Lessons of this type appear as a series of highly engaging activities that aim at mass practice with content or skill components without visible connectedness to the proficiency or measurable language of the target.

- **Content-focused lessons:** The focus of these lessons is to absorb as much content as possible. Lessons of this type appear, on the surface, to be connected with a target; however, upon closer examination, they simply digest or present information on a unit, theme, or topic and nothing more, asking students to amass facts and formulas for short-term application.

- **Aptitude-focused lessons:** The focus of these lessons is demonstration of knowledge. While these lessons appear as rich reflective discussions or passionate debates, they are mainly large-scale presentations that only attempt to *verify* learning, not to *promote* learning.

- **Product-focused lessons:** The focus of these lessons is a hands-on creation of a product. These lessons appear to achieve high levels of engagement but lack reflective components. The lessons become an arbitrary list of to-do items that are connected to the *verb* of the target instead of the proficiency aspects.

In true proficiency-based instructional planning, teachers align *all* student tasks toward the proficiency-based learning target. By placing the measurable language of the target at the center of the instructional plan, lesson delivery and execution will be directly tied to the proficiency expectation. An example of the effect that non-proficiency has on planning is featured in figure 1.3. In this example, a class lesson or unit was planned around a learning target that does not contain a proficiency expectation: *Students will be able to explain the causes of World War I.* As proficiency is not at the center of the instructional planning process in this example, the unit plan and the daily teaching represent activities in search of a purpose.

Explain the causes of World War I.

Figure 1.3: Lesson plan for a nonproficiency-based target.

In the planning example in figure 1.3, we see the fill-in-the-blank sections inserted superficially, simply to gain a psychometric (feel-good) measure of whether the students know the content, and given that the expectation of how well a student should know the content is not clearly defined, students can *explain* in any way they want.

If we look at the same learning target in a *proficiency*-based lesson (figure 1.4), we see a dramatic shift from the types of activities in the traditional lesson example in figure 1.3. We also see a very well-defined and developed lesson connected to the proficiency-based learning target. Not only can the students now identify a proficiency expectation but it is now also unmistakably observable to anyone in the classroom.

Using examples from class, [students will be able to] effectively explain the main causes of World War I in a written analysis.

Figure 1.4: Lesson plan for a proficiency-based target.

In this proficiency-based planning example, students know not only that they have to write but also that they are required to use *only* examples from class and map out the *main* causes—not all of them.

This planning around proficiency results in a dynamic environment with a high sense of purpose of what is being learned and how well it has to be learned. In figure 1.4's example, learning is not pointed toward content, skills, or themes but noticeably pointed toward an intention and outcome of proficiency.

Focusing All Resources on a Proficiency Expectation

In proficiency-based instruction, we are continually deploying strategies and resources to react to, respond to, and reinforce the reflective process of students. The strategic and continual implementation of strategies and resources tied to a proficiency expectation facilitates learning sequences that help students answer the question, "How well do I need to know this?" and help teachers focus all aspects of the lesson on the proficiency-based learning target. Every opening activity; all teacher questions; all student responses; all engagement in individual student work, group work, whole-class and small-group discussion; and all teacher feedback must be focused on the measurable pieces of a proficiency-based target.

By intentionally directing our instructional focus toward measurable proficiency levels, student learning shifts from an individual internalization of knowledge and skills to a collaborative facilitation and development of student thought and reflection patterns. Consider the example of a high school health teacher we recently worked with. The teacher shared with us that in previous years only 39 percent of his students each semester passed the Red Cross CPR aptitude exam. After a few moments of discussion, we asked about his learning target. He stated that his target was *To identify the oxygen rescue steps and explain how to use them.* The conversation continued to focus on the instructional strategies that he was using in class, and he stated he tirelessly organizes elaborate lesson structures to support his students. As we talked, we found that although he was working ridiculously hard to help students be successful in relation to the learning target, for years he had been getting the same result—students consistently fell short of the intended learning outcomes—and by big numbers. As a teacher who cared deeply about his students and their learning, he was frustrated, tired, and unsure of how to move forward.

After instructional coaching, peer support, and collaborative conversations centered on keeping the instructional focus in all class activities on proficiency ("How well do I need to know this?"), the teacher changed the learning target to *I can accurately explain all the oxygen rescue steps in their appropriate sequence.* Using the proficiency-based instructional model, he then organized each section of his lesson around the new proficiency-based learning target. When we followed up with the teacher later in the semester to check in and see how his students were doing with the new proficiency-based learning targets and the instructional activities focusing on student reflection, our teacher was simply stunned by the results. With a tear in his eye, he explained the instructional planning and delivery that he employed in class, and he described the ways in which students reflected on their learning and how for the first time in his twenty-year career, 100 percent of his students passed the CPR exam on the first attempt.

The deliberate employment of resources toward a proficiency-based target has immense educational value and should appear as rigorous engagement related to the intended learning target. When a teacher employs proficiency-based instructional strategies, students engage in learning by constantly attempting to clarify proficiency, by testing new thinking without the fear of failing, and by challenging their emerging patterns of competency.

Regardless of how well developed a learning target may be, an instructional lesson can easily veer down the wrong road if we do not keep proficiency at the center of our instruction. As we do this, we develop a proficiency awareness that permeates everything that we do during the beginning, middle, and end of class. To illustrate, let's first review a lesson plan (figure 1.5) that does *not* keep proficiency at the center of instruction.

Using examples from class, students will be able to effectively explain the main causes of World War I in a written analysis.

Figure 1.5: Nonproficiency-based lesson plan.

When we focus instruction on the proficiency language of the target, we get a much different lesson. As we can see in the next example (figure 1.6), a lesson that is focused on proficiency has an observable and deliberate purpose that allows students to transfer developing skills along the gradual scaling of competency, from left to right, between sections of the lesson.

Using examples from class, students will be able to effectively explain the main causes of World War I in a written analysis.

Figure 1.6: Proficiency-based lesson plan.

If the lesson lacks a clear articulation of proficiency, it drastically changes the classroom lesson or unit of study, leaving learning to be disconnected, exhausting, and unfulfilling. Both teacher and student are left scrambling to digest disparate elements of content and skill. This scrambling often perpetuates the need for giant review packets, constant reteaching, and countless tutoring sessions before or after school.

As teachers experiment with instructional practices that incorporate a proficiency expectation, we see mobilizing resources toward proficiency that are essential to providing students with experiences that focus on mastery of the intended targets. To make the experience for students even more powerful, teachers can create learning events that support a proficiency expectation.

Creating Learning Events That Support a Proficiency Expectation

We saw in the previous section that all events must relate to a proficiency-based target; however, in order to support this learning environment *all events* must also relate to each other. In order to develop proficiency, a student must experience that proficiency early and often through reflective and formative assessment. Think about it this way: if I am going to make a big speech to my colleagues, I would find it prudent to practice my speech in the following five steps.

1.   Recite speech out loud in my room

2.   Recite speech to mirror

3.   Recite speech to family member

4.   Recite speech to a few friends

5.   Recite speech to colleagues

It must be no different in proficiency-based instruction; proficiency-based assessments must relate to proficiency-based instruction in order to produce proficiency-based feedback. That is to say that both instruction and assessment must focus on the same proficiency-based target in order for students to develop and grow their competency. The problem is many of us just focus our assessment experiences on the proficiency-based target and forget to connect the instructional practice.

Take for example this lesson in which a teacher was using this target: *I can independently create an appropriate spoken message in familiar and unstructured situations.* When we spoke with this teacher about how she taught it, she answered with the following list of activities.

*   Students lead presentations on a given content topic.

*   Students present an original writing to the class.

*   Students create a product and present to groups.

*   Students make a time line of events and present to the class.

*   Students present a self-created collage of media that represent a given content topic.

As the teacher finished sharing this list, we asked her, "How do students prepare for these experiences?" She responded with full and well-thought-out descriptions of engaging activities that developed content knowledge about the topic of the unit. She also added that she uses formative assessments to gauge where the students are at a given point in each experience.

All this appeared to be well connected to the proficiency-based target, *I can independently create an appropriate spoken message in familiar and unstructured situations* since all the activities are in fact collecting evidence on a central idea of *oral presentation* proficiency. However, a problem arose when we asked this same teacher about the types of formative assessments and practice she uses to prepare the students for these assessment experiences. She responded with the following list.

- Content-based quizzes (written and oral)
- Peer-to-peer argumentative discussions (guided and unguided)
- Free-response writing (both short answers and long argument)
- Videos and multimedia
- Short-response homework, warm-ups, and exit slips answering essential contextual questions

What we noticed about this instructional list is that it is not really preparing the students for the target *I can independently create an appropriate spoken message in familiar and unstructured situations.* How can a student attempt to develop proficiency on *creating an independent spoken message* when he or she is writing free-response questions, passively taking notes on a video, or taking a matching or selected-response quiz on the content?

During the entire conversation we had with this teacher, she spoke with conviction and passion about her students, and we don't want to disregard the hours that it took to plan a lesson such as this; however, in the second list—the instructional list—students were hardly being prepared for the target at all! It is no wonder that students see learning as a disconnected series of events (Black & Wiliam, 1998).

In the teacher's first list of activities, all items clearly relate to each other. However, the assessment experiences in the second list must relate to the events in the first list to be proficiency based. The reason this is important is that students must be able to engage in events that are promoting the intended proficiency! Without this, students will fail to see purpose in the learning, fail to take notice on their emerging proficiency, and fail to create new learning from feedback.

So how can we get the list of activities to relate to the list of assessments? We can create this connection in the following three ways.

1. Pick an assessment event that relates to the proficiency-based target.
2. Create a new smaller-scale version of the original event by asking what is a similar yet more digestible way for students to experience it.

3. Take the new smaller-scale version and make it a formative practice for students.

After discussing this approach with the teacher from the previous scenario, we saw her list-one items merge with list two.

1. Pick an assessment event that relates to the proficiency-based target. Students:

    a. Give student-led presentations on a given content topic

    b. Present an original writing to the class

    c. Create a product and present to groups

    d. Make a time line of events and present to the class

    e. Make a collage of media that represent a given content topic

2. Create a new smaller-scale version of the original event by asking what is a similar yet more digestible way for students to experience it.

    a. Students pick a topic from a hat and present to a shoulder partner using the resources they have at their disposal.

    b. Students bring in an article and present to groups of students.

    c. Students choose an image of a product and present to small groups.

    d. Teacher provides guided questions as students discuss a time line of events.

    e. Teacher provides three collages, and students discuss in small groups which version best represents a given topic.

3. Take the new smaller-scale version and make it a formative practice for students.

    a. Partner uses rubric with performance criteria to offer feedback to peer.

    b. Each group gets to ask one question or give one tip to presenter to help clarify his or her delivery and speech.

    c. Students work together to sell their product to the larger class.

    d. Students record themselves talking about a chosen time line and share recording with teacher for feedback.

    e. Students create a collage of an event or content topic, and class performs a gallery walk where students present collages and provide feedback simultaneously.

When these steps are taken and both assessment and instruction experiences are connected to each other through the proficiency-based target, students can engage in potent formative assessment learning, feel free to act on feedback without the fear of failure, try out new thoughts or strategies, begin to observe and reflect in much more meaningful ways on emerging proficiency, and, most important, increase the quality of their work.

In proficiency-based instruction, since all events in this process are based on a singular proficiency and not a random mix of thematically related pieces, the students can act on feedback, validate new thoughts or learning, and experientially reflect on emerging proficiency. As Amanda Ripley (2013) states in *The Smartest Kids in the World: And How They Got That Way*, "Students meet the expectation you set for them" (p. 441), so what we are saying is that the primary goal of proficiency-based assessment is to set proficiency expectations *high* and relate *everything* to it.

Element 3: Proficiency-Based Reflection

Over the years we have become more and more convinced that really good assessment can be more accurately thought of as really good *reflection*. When we consider reflection in a traditional assessment model, we hear from colleagues that reflection is usually a concluding experience at the end of a lesson or unit of instruction. While considering what we typically call *formative assessment*, we often hear that the purpose of reflection is for teachers and students to interpret results and guide next steps. Our feeling, however, is that we need to develop a new understanding of the power of reflection and its proper place in the assessment cycle. The fact that most reflection in the traditional teaching and learning cycle occurs near the end of a lesson or unit of instruction limits the reflective process from becoming a valuable instructional tool in and of itself.

In proficiency-based assessment, we view reflection as something much more significant than responses and simple questions such as "How am I doing?" or "Where am I with my learning?" To reorder our thinking and practices regarding assessment, we offer three components of what we call proficiency-based reflection: the act of examining one's current state of competency in relation to a gradation of learning and considering potential next steps to further understanding.

1. Repurposing reflection events as assessments

2. Having students create reflective statements

3. Increasing student feedback acceptance (Ilgen, Fisher, & Taylor, 1979)

Repurposing Reflection Events as Assessments

As we move into a proficiency-based reflection model, it is important to remember that good reflection *is* assessment and good assessment *is* reflection. Designed and implemented correctly, proficiency-based reflection opportunities are more effective than any traditional test or assessment a teacher can give a student. A reflection event that acts as an assessment is a much more personalized and meaningful learning event. Simultaneously, the reflection provides pivotal feedback for teachers to guide instruction and growth feedback to students as those reflections are tied to crystal clear proficiency-based targets. A teacher that we have worked with on proficiency-based assessment stated after shifting her practice toward proficiency-based reflection, "I care more about where my *students* think they are in their learning than where *I* think they are."

This is not a subtle distinction. When students are provided with the tools to consistently, and in real time, reflect on their learning in relation to the proficiency expectation, learning gains are significant. When reflection is rooted in and tied to a proficiency expectation, we create a meaningful interplay between the student, the lesson, and the proficiency-based learning target. Consider the following example.

First, the teacher asks students to answer the following question.

> At the end of the play *Romeo and Juliet*, Romeo wrongly thinks that Juliet is dead. He kills himself, and when Juliet awakes, she is shocked and despairing. She infers as to why he took his own life. What can the reader infer about the reason Shakespeare ends this play with this tragic misunderstanding?

Then, the students produce an answer such as the following.

> By the end of the play *Romeo and Juliet*, the reader should infer one of Shakespeare's running themes that sometimes only tragedy can end a long-lasting grudge. Throughout the entire play, we hear this message stated explicitly. The play opens with a prologue that warns the reader about the fate of Romeo and Juliet, and it recognizes that only through the tragedy of their deaths is the family's historical grudge repaired.

Next, instead of showing a model to the students, the teacher asks the students to record what they think about their finished product and record their thoughts on the rubric in figure 1.7.

While we see many reflective activities stop here, this teacher continued on with asking students to now view different work—not telling them if it was good or bad—and asked the students to decide which one of the exemplars their work was most similar to. One exemplar she provided is as follows.

Use the following rubric to assess your response for the two learning target areas.

	4 Exceeds	3 Meets	2 Approaching Mastery	1 Still Developing
Inferences / Key Details	Analysis reflects detailed insight into complex relationships.	Analysis reflects complete detailed insight into complex stated relationships.	Analysis reflects complete detailed insight into simple stated relationships.	Analysis reflects limited detailed insight into simple stated relationships.
Textual Evidence	Evidence is strong and creative to support what the text says as well as inferences.	Evidence is strong and thorough to support what the text says as well as inferences.	Evidence is strong and supports what the text says as well as inferences.	Evidence is strong and supports what the text says.

Reflect: In your own words, explain why you scored your response as you did and how you might attempt to reach the next level.

Figure 1.7: Sample proficiency-based reading rubric.

> By the end of the play *Romeo and Juliet*, the reader should infer one
> of Shakespeare's running themes: Sometimes only tragedy can end a
> long-lasting grudge. Throughout the entire play, we hear this message
> stated explicitly. The play opens with a prologue that warns the reader
> about the fate of Romeo and Juliet. The prologue comments on Romeo
> and Juliet's misadventures, "Whole misadventured piteous overthrows /
> Do with their death bury their parents' strife" (Prologue 7–8). Here, at the
> beginning of the story, we are told how the lasting "ancient grudge" will
> end. At the end of the play, when Romeo wrongly thinks Juliet is dead
> and kills himself, the reader is shocked by the tragic mistake. This tragedy
> is then heightened when Juliet's despair pushes her to end her own life,
> by her own hand (Act 5, Scene 3). The loss to both families solidifies the
> message behind the relationship between pain and reconciliation.

Lastly, the teacher asks the students to identify which gradations of the proficiency-based target they are on and also how they will attempt to get to the next gradation, prompting, "When you reflected on how to reach the next level, did your response accurately reflect what you saw in the models from one level to the next?"

In traditional assessment and reflection models, we would see quite the opposite from the previously featured exemplar. We would more than likely see a teacher vigorously engaging students in instructional activities, and then, only after the activities were wrapping up, would he or she provide opportunities for reflection. As we move toward an assessment model based on proficiency, we must come to see that reflection and assessment are the *same thing*, and when done well, reflective opportunities for students are tied to proficiency-based learning targets.

Having Students Create Reflective Statements

In a proficiency-based assessment model, reflection opportunities must be designed to help students discover answers to questions that are born out of their interaction with the proficiency expectation. The following questions can help guide students' reflection and help them develop a deeper understanding of the proficiency expectation and their current state of competency.

- "How is my work beginning to emerge in the expected level of proficiency?"

- "How am I attempting to transfer skills and knowledge between gradations of the proficiency-based target?"

- "Can I distinguish between my work and the exemplar for each gradation of the target?"

In order for students to answer these emerging questions we must help them develop a *proficiency awareness*—a student's personal interpretation of his or her current state of competency in relationship to a gradation of learning. We can support students' development of proficiency awareness by helping them create proficiency testimonials. These clear, detailed written statements help students identify the knowledge and skills they have been asked to master, clarify the level of proficiency they expect to attain, and identify steps on how to reach the next level of proficiency. Most importantly, they serve as a wonderful metacognitive opportunity that allows students to examine their own thinking.

With proficiency-based reflection, recording proficiency and secondary action statements becomes an essential experience for learning. Let's look at our healthy target from earlier: *Using examples from class, students will be able to effectively explain the main political, economic, and social causes of World War I in a written analysis.* Examples of proficiency testimonials related to this target include "I need to review the economic differences between the involved countries because I didn't think the economic situation was causing problems" and "I need to include more detail in my example of the death of Franz Ferdinand, because that seems to be the cause of the war."

While we recognize that many students may be spending time reflecting on their learning, if they are doing so with unhealthy targets, we question the helpfulness of the activity. When using an unhealthy target that does not contain proficiency, measurability, or gradation of learning, students can only create vague reflective statements that sound more like to-do list items, such as "I really need to review those vocabulary words tonight" or "I need to work harder on the readings, because the content is harder than I thought." In statements such as these, it is evident that the target is missing proficiency language, as students are unable to reflect successfully, and they focus more on work to be completed and less on proficiency. Examples where we can see ambiguity in students' reflective thinking as a result of the nonproficiency-based target *Students will be able to explain the causes of World War I* include the following: "I need to add more details to my explanation about World War I" and "I have to review the social causes more, focusing on the imperialistic nature of involved countries."

We can see in these statements students struggling to produce any valuable reflection for either themselves or the teacher. These testimonials also lack clarity and action, as seen through the nebulous prescriptive language of "add more" or the worried and desperate language of "have to." Ultimately, students will view this product as an unreliable aid to their learning. This ambiguity happens when the target and resulting instruction lack a proficiency expectation.

In the proficiency-based examples, students are able to clarify their thinking around the proficiency language of the target, which causes reflection to become an integral part of the instructional and learning experiences. Students as well as teachers should be able to look at the data these reflective testimonials produce and easily verify that a student is growing, learning, and demonstrating emerging elements of proficiency.

Increasing Student Feedback Acceptance

As formative assessment is becoming more and more popular and talked about in the educational literature, we have heard educators discuss the need for assessment practices that facilitate the collection of meaningful data and feedback for themselves and their students. While we often hear thoughtful articulation of what good assessment should look like, in many cases, once it is implemented, students do not see the data and feedback as helpful tools. Instead, we hear students that we work with tell us that the data serve more as a litmus test of whether they know or can do something—a toggle switch that must be flipped from off to on. In describing this experience, students often make remarks such as, "When we get the test back to review, I can see which targets I got right, and which ones that I got wrong, but I am not really sure what to do next." As a result, students are often unaware that the feedback can be an instructional tool and instead look to see the impact that the assessment will have on their grades.

The last thing that we want is for students to see reflection as a task to be completed—or worse, another grade to be compiled. This may occur because the stakes for assessments are sometimes too high, the material can be too dense, the lessons may be disconnected from a proficiency expectation, or there may be little to no incentive for students to participate in reflective-thinking activities. We believe that this lack of feedback acceptance leads to low student responsibility in the learning process.

As we create learning opportunities that help students understand the relationship between feedback and the proficiency-based learning targets, students will begin to see the value of the reflection experiences and come to see that their own learning and development are directly tied to the frequency and quality of their reflective experiences. To increase feedback acceptance among students, we need to create assessment events that help students see that:

- Assessment is about making connections, not making right answers
- Assessment is an *active* search for meaning
- Assessment is developmental, not fixed
- Assessment is a thinking activity requiring collaboration and deliberation
- Assessment is *using* knowledge, not *verifying* knowledge

Proficiency-based assessment is not a wild departure from what we currently know and do as teachers. While these changes may be significant for some teachers and small for others, they are having a huge impact on student learning and achievement. As we work with teachers who are learning and implementing proficiency-based assessment, we continue to believe that the traditional models of professional development are indeed outdated and a new strategy for teacher learning must emerge.

Key Points

Following are key points from the chapter that readers should review to ensure they have a firm grasp on the content.

- When targets contain proficiency and measurability and reflect a gradation of learning, they become extremely powerful and dynamic instructional tools—so much so that assessment becomes nothing more than a reaction to student-produced evidence in relation to a proficiency-based target.

- In proficiency-based instruction, teachers use intentional strategies to initiate and monitor students' own ability to create *active* solutions to any identified learning gaps, all while generating clarity of the content.

- With proficiency-based assessment, recording reflections and making secondary action statements based on feedback increase the chances that students will accept and act on the feedback from the teacher or a peer.

Chapter 2

Preparation

Although school leaders may work diligently to prepare for each professional development event, we often hear from school leaders that the professional development becomes a stand-alone event with little follow-through. This chapter is designed to examine and suggest ways in which we first prepare educators for change prior to actually implementing change through professional development. Then, as we progress, we build supportive strategies that institutionalize positive changes for teacher collaboration and student learning.

Preparing individuals for change goes beyond communication strategies. It goes much deeper to build the internal structure and the intricate architecture needed to support change in a more sturdy and steady way. This step in the change process takes time, but it is worth every invested minute.

Every journey begins by preparing to go. If you are going on a long trip, you make checklists and plans, think ahead, create an itinerary, and pack carefully to make sure you have everything from your plane tickets to your toothbrush. Preparing for implementing a change in schools requires the same attention to detail. It requires that you organize, make sure all parties have what they need in order to move forward, have an itinerary, and have a mindset that acknowledges traveling rarely goes as planned. That said, we prepare as best as we can.

Preparing for change is one of the most often overlooked and underdeveloped efforts in professional learning. Following are three key points to remember during the preparation stage.

1. The collaborative team members need to be willing to question and challenge their current practices in order to develop more effective strategies to ensure success for every student.

2. The collaborative team members must be able to develop consensus and a shared commitment to improving their individual and collective practices in order to move forward.

3. All team members must fully understand why they are being asked to consider a change in their traditional practices.

As you read the following story about a team beginning to develop curriculum around proficiency-based assessment, consider the ways in which the team members first prepare for change, learning, and investigating; ask questions; and flesh out each other's understanding. In doing so, the team engages in the powerful work of collaborative teams and learns more together. Listen to the characters. They represent a wide variety of mindsets—some early adopters, some willing to change, some questioning change, and some really holding back. However, each teacher is a change agent. When reading, ask yourself the following questions: "What does each individual change agent need? How do you as a leader support teachers in their efforts early in the change process? How is confidence toward change developing?"

As you read the team's story, pay attention to the following items as the team comes to better understand and prepare for proficiency-based assessment.

•   Individuals on a team understand the differences and benefits of proficiency-based assessment over traditional formative and summative assessment practices; all team members must have an agreed-on working knowledge.

•   Proficiency-based assessments are dependent on effectively written targets.

•   The team members reach out for support and guidance as they learn new strategies that challenge old assumptions.

Our Team's Story

At the end of the year, Eisenhower School's team of teacher leaders met up to reflect on the year's work and to discuss plans for the upcoming year. They collaborated with administrators at the school to problem solve and to think about better ways to support teaching and learning. One of the long-standing challenges at Eisenhower has been change. For years, attempts at professional learning and change have felt like a series of false starts—the discussion of good ideas got started, but ideas were never implemented. Other teacher leaders reflected that professional learning and change were presented as a one-size-fits-all remedy—as if all teachers and all teacher teams needed the exact same support. This end-of-the-year meeting was meant to address those two concerns.

Eisenhower's faculty were hard working, but the team leaders and administrators recognized that approaches to professional learning and change were often unclear and frustrating to teachers. This year, the teacher team leaders and administrators decided to make clear commitments around how professional learning and change might be more meaningful and better integrated into teaching and learning practices. They wanted to make sure that they supported professional learning experiences that would be inquiry based and tailored to each teacher and each team's specific needs. After all, they recognized that some teachers were veteran experts, and some were only just getting started in their teaching careers—and, of course, there was a great variety of experience in between. Likewise, some teachers were optimistic about change while others questioned change and its value. These two variables demand different approaches to professional learning and growth. The challenge for this meeting was to structure a model that would differentiate professional learning in a way that not only prepared teachers for meaningful change but also worked to solicit input and collaboration around the integration of change. As one teacher leader put it, "We all need to remember that change is a process, not just a product that can be put in place."

With this in mind, the teacher leaders and administrators decided to adopt an approach to professional learning as if they were entering into a creative process. Adapted from the long-standing research on creativity—synthesized by Mihaly Csikszentmihalyi (1990)—Eisenhower School decided to approach professional learning by concentrating on the five phases Csikszentmihalyi outlines: (1) preparation, (2) incubation, (3) insight, (4) evaluation, and (5) elaboration to help construct differentiated professional learning opportunities for teachers and teams—providing the support they need at different phases of change.

The architects of this approach acknowledged that teachers and teams are always in different places in the creative process. Often, professional learning is about *preparing* teachers for a change; for others, it should provide time to *incubate* and think about change possibilities. For some teams, they need professional learning that works to reach aha! moments and *insights* from their collective expertise. Furthermore, professional learning might require structured time to *evaluate* teaching and learning practices or for the teacher or teacher team to attain the support to revise an idea, nuance the idea, or *elaborate* on the idea.

Bruce, a team leader for the social studies department, was excited about this differentiated approach. He recognized the value of working with teachers to support them individually, and he wanted a professional learning structure that valued everyone's input. Bruce directed his thinking to each area of this process, and how he might approach preparation differently from the phases of incubation, insight, evaluation, and elaboration. He noted to himself how these phases interact, and he noted that each of his team members might not all be in the same phase at the same time. For Bruce, making changes in his team had been construed as clunky and top down. He wanted to build change based on the involvement and commitment of his team and members' expertise. He wanted to foster clarity, commitment, collaboration, and coherence among his colleagues as they worked to build better decisions for teaching and learning.

Including Bruce, there were five teachers on the team. This was Vaughn's first year. She was very excited to be on the team and knew she had a lot to learn from the other team teachers. Joni, a long-time veteran teacher, would mentor Vaughn this year. She was equally enthusiastic about the idea to approach change in a more integrated way. Morrison had been on the team for twenty-five years, bringing with him a unique perspective and a wealth of experience. Britney was the fifth team member. She had taught for a few years and was working really hard to make some changes in her practice. She questioned and reflected on each decision she made—a valuable strength to the team.

That afternoon, Bruce sketched out a professional learning framework (figure 2.1) that helped him visualize the new process the school was embracing, showing each stage and how there are various different paths between each stage that the team members could move between.

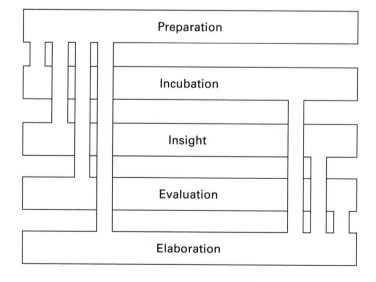

Figure 2.1: Professional learning framework sketch.

He noted that phases would and should overlap, different teachers on the same team might be in different phases, and each phase required a different leadership support, reflection, and consideration. The framework worked to support both inquiry and decision making about proficiency-based assessment. Bruce thought about how his team could make use of the framework as they were embarking on their efforts to integrate work around proficiency-based assessment—a significant team change from the traditional practices at Eisenhower. He looked forward to collaboration with his colleagues, but he also knew that his team was hesitant about integrating proficiency-based assessment, that they still had a lot of questions about its purpose, and they wondered what kind of effect it would have on students. Moreover, there would be a new teacher on the team this year, and there were also teachers who had been on the team for more than fifteen years. Bruce thought about his goal to support different teachers with different professional learning; he thought about each teacher's strengths and about his commitment to building team decisions with these strengths.

Before beginning the preparation phase of the team's work, Bruce wanted the team to clearly and fully understand the rationale for the change to proficiency-based assessment and he wanted to make sure his team was clear on the *why* behind the change, that everyone could define the change, and that the change to proficiency-based assessment was worth their collaborative time dedicated to improving teaching and learning.

He explained that the framework was there to help the team pay attention to the change process, instead of the one-size-fits-all model members were used to. The effort for the year would be to create protocols for professional learning that would support the progression of understanding and decision making for integrating proficiency-based assessment, which encouraged developing this concept through the investigation of new ideas, challenging dialogue, inventiveness, and reflection.

He said, "This is meant to be a process to create change in a meaningful, thought-out way—not just to institute a change. Instead, the professional learning framework is meant to be a way to guide the integration of proficiency-based assessment as it best suits the needs of teaching and learning. I'd like for us to work together in a way that views change as a process, not just a product we want to put in place."

Bruce explained the learning framework more fully, outlining the purposes of each phase, and he clarified how each phase had equal value and how phases often overlapped. He shared the reasoning behind adopting the approach, and he answered members' questions about how he would structure the team's work—with their help—around each phase of preparation, incubation, insight, evaluation, and elaboration. Bruce reasserted that the professional learning framework was a way to support collaboration around their professional practices. He made it clear that the effort for their meetings would be to solicit the viewpoints and ideas from their collective expertise.

As Bruce explained, he reintroduced the concept of proficiency-based assessment to his team as a way of preparing the team for future discussions. He noted, "The commitment we made for the year is to rethink the relationship between assessment and curriculum and instruction. Our main focus for this work is to develop practices where proficiency-based assessment directly places the learner's proficiency at the center of all we do and say as educators." Bruce outlined how each phase of the professional learning framework contains indicators of proficiency-based assessment: targets, instruction, and reflection. He explained that teams would use the framework to process their discussion and progress the work they were doing for students. Bruce highlighted, "The idea is to increase collaborative input and decision-minded discussions throughout the process of change. The framework is a guide, and each phase is equally important in helping us understand where we are in creating the change toward proficiency-based assessment."

Bruce knew the team was diverse, and he knew each member would need help collaborating around this change. Bruce was eager to get started and jump in; however, he decided to move more slowly at first. He resisted the impulse to make change happen overnight. He reminded himself that everyone on the team needed to be prepared first.

Bruce began the team meeting by saying, "Why don't we talk about how we will know we are all clear on and prepared for the basics of proficiency-based assessment. I want to make sure that we all have a shared understanding of why we would move in this direction, how we might proceed to integrate the work into our teaching practices, and what we will need to do in order to be effective for students. Our goal today is to make sure we've set up a plan that demonstrates we all understand proficiency-based assessment, that we share the same vision, and that we have clarity around what we are doing. I know it's been a long summer, but at the end of the year we had some training on proficiency-based assessment. Let's take some time to review and reflect on what we remember from that training, and let's make sure we all have a strong and shared working understanding."

As the meeting began, Joni brought up a number of observations and realizations. She always liked being a progressive adopter to anything that the team pursued. She started the discussion by saying, "Reviewing this learning framework, I would agree that we are still in the preparation stage based on this set of indicators. I don't think I have too many opinions right now because I can honestly only remember a few things from last year. I've thought about those ideas over the summer. Some I like, and some I don't understand. So, I'd benefit from a review session." The others agreed. In terms of proficiency-based assessment, they were only just getting started on how learning targets, instruction, and reflection worked together to achieve positive outcomes for students.

Smiling, Bruce said, "Well, I'm glad we are being honest with ourselves. When it comes to change, there is a lot to just learn and to discuss. It sounds like—as a team—we should allow ourselves some time to make better sense of proficiency-based assessment. As this is happening, let's make it a norm that we are patient with one another, listen to one another, and help each other along this process as we are making decisions. Undoubtedly, we will all start thinking in different phases at different times. For instance, I'll admit sometimes I start evaluating something without even trying it first!"

Morrison said, "Well Bruce, I'm never too old to change. I think you're right. This framework can help us to pace our collaboration if we respect each other's thinking and opinions. I like the norm. We will all have thoughts to consider with this change, but we will need to work together if we want to improve student achievement here."

Joni agreed and said, "This has got me thinking about why so many initiatives have come and gone without sticking. Maybe this framework will help us build a change that will last and help students. It is important for all of us to first really understand what we are trying to do in relation to proficiency-based assessment; I think we need to take some time to review our first unit's targets, exams, and assessments. Reviewing what we already do can help us see what we need to learn, what we need to revise, and what we need to change."

To Bruce's surprise, Vaughn, the newly hired first-year teacher, opened by wondering, "That would be really helpful for me. For instance, I'm struggling to understand some of the learning targets. Some of them are written in a way that I don't really understand. I'm not sure what skills my students are to learn. It would be great if we could spend some time on that area of our work."

Bruce asked Vaughn to continue. "Can you help us understand what you mean?"

Vaughn thought for a moment. "Well, we all agreed the preparation stage helps us to review our current practices, correct? As I went through the learning targets, I'm not sure I see them being a gradation of learning, which is what proficiency-based assessment needs to be. It would help me and our students if we all knew what everyone's thoughts were on the difference between *approaching* and *proficiency* and *mastery* of each target; otherwise, I think we will all be holding students to different standards."

Britney agreed with Vaughn. "I'm sure I could learn a lot from Joni and Morrison about these differences, too. Now that I've been teaching this class for a couple of years, I would benefit from calibrating my view of *mastery* to everyone else's view."

Morrison said, "In twenty-five years, I've never had that conversation with another teacher. I thought writing the targets was enough, but I think both of you are right. For instance, one of our targets is *Identify and explain the causes of World War I*. I think it's a specific target that works just fine because my students perform well each year in this unit, but I wonder what all of you think."

Britney added, "Right. It's the same with our summative exam. Even on our formative assessments, we as teachers can see that our students understand the target. It seems like we are doing a great job with our current targets, but we've never discussed the results in relation to proficiencies."

Placing several articles and readings on the table, Joni reinforced Britney's concern, "I see your point, Britney. Last week I reviewed the literature on proficiency-based assessment and gradations of learning. Even outside proficiency-based assessment, I found a lot of literature about learning progressions and scaling learning. I don't think we do that very well, and I think we could learn a lot from each other if we did."

Reviewing some of the articles Joni brought in for the team, Britney added, "There are a lot of terms I don't think we use accurately, and I can't seem to understand all these formative principles that we are being asked to understand. I have a friend who is a teacher at another school, and they refer to what we call targets as *learning outcomes*, and the Common Core refers to targets as *standards*, so I am confused about what all these terms mean." Morrison and Joni nodded that they felt the same way.

Bruce said, "Well, let's work in a way that really makes sense to us, and in a way that will make sense to students. I know there are a lot of terms, so I spent time this summer trying to summarize and clarify. It's not as hard to follow once you look at the curricular hierarchy." Bruce provided his team with a handout that articulated each level of the hierarchy as follows.

Level 1: What is your course about? What are the big ideas?

Level 2: What is being assessed?

Level 3: How well is a student expected to demonstrate the skills in level 2?

Level 4: What are the conditions for success?

Bruce began again, "Level 1, the highest level, represents the big pillars of the class, such as reading, writing, interpretive skills, technique, and so on. Level 2 (one level down) communicates what the class is doing, such as writing an essay, identifying poetry terms, or determining a key detail from a text. The third level must communicate how well students need to perform a skill, such as cite key details from textual evidence to create and validate an argument or create arguments using historical context in an unstructured writing prompt. The fourth level identifies all the criteria or conditions we give a student to qualify the 'how well' of level 3. Think of them as a list of tools in a toolbox to complete the level 3 'how well' distinction."

"I'm not sure I fully understand," said Morrison.

Bruce reorganized his thoughts and presented the information with an analogy, "OK, follow me through this logic. Imagine you were about to go grocery shopping." Bruce proceeded to role-play with Morrison.

> **Bruce:** Can you go grocery shopping for me?
>
> **Morrison:** Yes . . . but what am I buying?
>
> **Bruce:** You are buying milk.
>
> **Morrison:** OK . . . well . . . what kind?
>
> **Bruce:** Whatever is the healthiest.
>
> **Morrison:** OK . . . but how do I know what is the healthiest?
>
> **Bruce:** Just compare and contrast each brand using your opinion, based on what you can gather from the label.
>
> **Morrison:** I still don't feel I can get the healthiest brand.
>
> **Bruce:** OK, here are the brands that you should compare and contrast—compare each label for its nutritional content and decide which brand is the healthiest to drink: Sunshine Farms, Green's Dairy, and Naturally Good. Just pick one after you review the label information.

When Bruce finished, Joni understood the point of the activity: to locate the target. "So where is the target in that story?" she asked.

Bruce continued, "Well, it could be to *compare and contrast brands of milk for health benefits using the label information.*"

Morrison quickly jumped in, "Wait. Why wouldn't it just be buying milk? That's what students have to do. It is very clear."

Bruce responded, "That's the real challenge in writing a good learning target. Buying milk can't easily be made into a gradation of learning, so it is not your target."

Morrison said, "So . . ."

Bruce continued, "Let me outline our conversation this way by using the simple levels I mentioned earlier. Level 1 is grocery shopping. Level 2 is buying milk. Level 3 is comparing and contrasting brands for health benefit using opinion and label information. Level 4 is analyzing fat content, calcium level, and potential hormones."

Joni quickly added, "So level 3 is our target, not level 2, buying milk."

Britney added, "Why are level 4s not targets? They are the most specific." Vaughn seemed to agree with her.

Bruce explained, "Level 4 contains the building blocks—both content and skills—that a student needs to possess in order to satisfy the target."

Bruce provided another comparison, "Think about it this way," he said. "If I were to ask you to build a house, I would not teach you what a hammer is first, then a nail, then drywall, then wood, and so on. I would ask you to build a house, hand you all the tools necessary for building a house, and have you reflect on which ones you need help with in building the house. I would assess you on how well you build a house, not how well you understand the hammer or how well you know the dimensions of a nail. The dimensions of a nail and the skill of using a hammer are not targets but rather criteria or prerequisite learning essential to building a house."

Bruce continued, "So as I understand it, the target is level 3, but it seems like our targets are either at level 2, what students need to do, or even at level 4."

Vaughn said, "If we work on that, I think I would be able to teach much more effectively." Bruce agreed too, "I see what you are saying. Now they don't seem right to me either, and they certainly don't represent a gradation of learning."

Morrison added, "So our target for this unit, *Identify and explain the causes of World War I*, is not written correctly? Help me to understand."

Bruce responded, "The target really needs to have four gradations if we are going to work with a proficiency-based assessment model. Our target should be the third gradation. Gradation 4 is exceeding the expected target, gradation 3 is meeting the expected target, gradation 2 is approaching the expected target, and gradation 1 is not close to the expectation." At this point, Bruce showed them a visual he had sketched to more clearly show how all the pieces fit together (see figure 2.2). Bruce went on to explain, "Basically, there are four gradations that a student can occupy, which demonstrate how well he or she is doing, and the third gradation is the goal."

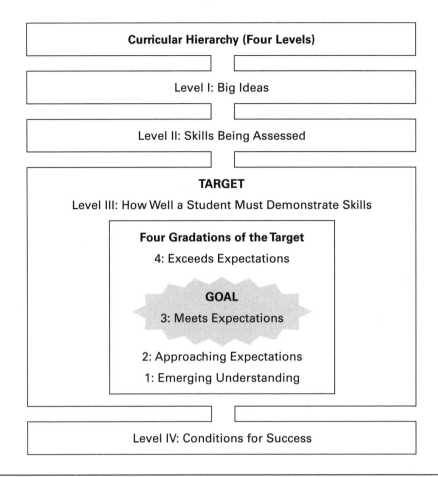

Figure 2.2: Overview of proficiency-based assessment curricular hierarchy components.

*Visit **go.solution-tree.com/assessment** for a reproducible version of this figure.*

Joni said, "I guess, if I think about it, our current percentage-based grading system of A, B, C, D, and F seems like a five-level gradation, doesn't it? But a D and F are really one category. Most schools, including ours, consider D ineligible. There are always four gradations of expectations."

"Or," Morrison pointed out, "I teach AP courses, and those have a very specific five-point gradation rubric. You can't get around that."

Bruce said, "Well, if you think about it, AP scores 2 and 1 don't earn a student college credit, so they are the same level really."

Morrison realized what he meant, saying, "I never really thought about it that way."

Britney, realizing that a change in the team's approach to targets was about to happen, added, "So what do we have to do now, rewrite all of our targets? That alone will take a lot of time. Think about all the time we have invested in proficiency-based assessment already. Where do we begin now?"

There was silence. The group was at a crossroads, and there was tension in the air. "Well," Bruce began, "one of the steps in getting to our goal of proficiency-based assessment is to make sure our learning targets represent a gradation of learning, a progression from simple to more complex content or skills. So I think we should just start there, making a gradation of our target from simple to more complex. In a lot of ways, I think this will help us to better prepare if we work collaboratively."

This led to a discovery by Morrison: "So essentially our targets need to represent four levels of mastery or a scaffold of complexity within a specific content or skill?"

And Britney noted that the group members likely already did this within their lesson planning. She said, "Essentially, we are collaborating to come to an agreement around what we consider to be the differences in the gradations of mastery, proficiency, approaching, and not close."

Bruce explained, "I think so. I think scaling our targets will help us to move through the preparation stage of learning because it will force us to collaborate over our learning expectations." The team agreed that reviewing the targets and the expectations of each target was the first real step toward the integration of proficiency-based assessment.

The team began with the World War I target. Working collaboratively, each member began scaling the target. After a relatively short period of time, the team produced the following set of gradations from simple to more complex.

1—I can identify the causes of World War I.

2—I can define the causes of World War I.

3—I can explain the causes of World War I.

4—I can analyze the causes of World War I.

"I love it!" said Joni. Although most of the group members felt they still had some work to do, they felt that this gradation of learning provided clarity in their lessons, communication, and feedback. Bruce decided to seize the success of the moment to bring the meeting to a close and outline action steps for the next meeting.

"With the few minutes we have left," Bruce said, "let's talk about what we have learned from this discussion, which by the way, has been the best conversation we've had in a while. Let's go around and state our takeaways. Joni, would you go first? You seemed the most excited about how our thinking is changing; can you tell us why?"

Joni proclaimed, "I never thought about targets being a gradation of learning. I always looked at them as what we expected students to do. Really, though, I just thought of them as a list of things a student must do or internalize to perform on a test." Joni then continued, "I can cognitively walk students up to a test in a clearer, more organized manner by remediating each of these tiers along the way."

Morrison stated, "The gradations make the expectations more specific, and if we collaborate, discuss, and decide on them, our students will be evaluated more equitably among our classes. This will help when we do our data analysis around common formative assessments. I'm thinking this will help us to have better discussions about teaching and learning."

Vaughn reflected, "I feel that students now will know where they are and where they are going, which should ultimately help them build skills that they are able to talk about and reflect over. I'd be excited if I heard students actually talking about learning more than talking about their grades."

Bruce added, "Yes. I didn't think about that. We could have students rank themselves where they fall on the scale. They could take more ownership over what they know and don't know."

Britney stated that the work in this direction sounded really worthwhile. She noted to the group, "Sharing our thoughts about the gradations of learning will help me develop more insights into teaching and learning. I'm already thinking about the insight phase though. I'm starting to have ideas about how this will help me."

As the meeting came to a close, Bruce asked the team to meet next week during the teachers' department time to finish scaling their first unit's targets. "Let's break our work into parts and not get overwhelmed. As we get better at this, it will get easier."

As his team left the room, Bruce sensed a heightened purpose growing. He couldn't remember a more productive meeting, and he was confident that his team had grown from the activity of scaling targets with communicated expectations. He would continue working with the team to revise their team targets and learning gradations that demonstrated student growth.

The Four Commitments of Proficiency-Based Assessment

In the preparation stage of team learning, team members must overcome specific challenges and problems that exist, problems created by fundamental gaps in curriculum, instruction, and assessment—or the concern that these three elements don't work together. In this stage of our journey, teams must first resolve central issues and build coherence and clarity to create a solid foundation from which to learn. Before a team can move forward, it must come to consensus on four commitments of proficiency-based assessment (Ainsworth & Viegut, 2006).

1. Establishing proficiency-based targets

2. Creating learning gradations

3. Using targets effectively in instruction

4. Developing assessment literacy

Commitment 1: Establishing Proficiency-Based Targets

One of the practices that we see quite often in schools is that standards, objectives, or learning targets are written in the syllabus, presented at the beginning of a lesson on the board, and used to guide assessment remediation. While it is important to do all of these things, when teachers use learning targets only in this way, they turn into nothing more than a checklist for particular content to be learned and skills to be formulaically mastered. This often creates a "get 'er done" culture in the classroom where teachers and students work diligently to check off each target and move to the next. When this happens, students are typically not required to think too deeply about higher-level questions and connections. This approach forces any meaningful conversation around proficiency out of the classroom and isolates teaching and learning to an outcomes-based experience (Schoemaker, 2011).

Outcomes-based learning can be defined as an environment focused solely on achievement instead of the thinking, planning, and reflection that precede achievement (Schoemaker, 2011). Outcomes-based learning can stifle student learning and reward bursts of aptitude—while at the same time ignoring thinking, reflection, and long-term patterns of growth (Schoemaker, 2011). When learning and thinking are ignored, students begin focusing on grades, collecting points, and satisfying the task at hand, while displaying high levels of anxiety for exams due to the focus on short-term retention of knowledge. Large formative and summative exams along with large review packets are the norm in outcomes-based classrooms, all with a heavy focus on content.

To help avoid outcomes-based environments, a learning target must be reworked to include *proficiency*. In other words, a target must spell out *how well* a teacher expects the students to learn the content or skill (Sandrock, 2011). Proficiency-based targets can be defined as four successive degrees (gradations) of competency that serve as measurable learning outcomes. Proficiency-based targets inherently ask the question, "How well is a student expected to demonstrate the new learning?" (Sandrock, 2011).

We have found that when teachers begin to develop instruction methods around learning targets that have proficiency expectations built in, the process of teaching and learning becomes a powerful interplay around thinking and growth and far less about content presentation and transfer. Furthermore, targets must embody high expectations of proficiency for all students, guiding and challenging students through inquiry and unrestricted learning experiences that allow them to grow.

Creating Proficiency-Based Learning Targets

As we stated in chapter 1, we know that within a collaborative team of teachers we must support one another in the writing of clear proficiency-based learning targets. However, even with the support of collaborative teams, it is easy for us to get stuck when creating targets. The following are essential questions a team of teachers can use to support one another when creating learning targets that are proficiency based. These questions help tease out the correct proficiency language to include in a learning target.

- What is my definition of quality for this topic?

- What does the end product look like?

- What is the purpose of this work?

- How will I measure this work?

What Is My Definition of Quality for This Topic?

When teachers are focused solely on their own version of quality, the ensuing conversation will help produce the proficiency and measurable language of a proficiency-based target. By asking teachers what they ideally want from students, words such as *effectively, consistently, in writing,* and so on are likely to be produced in the conversation. These proficiency-based keywords will create the foundation for a functional proficiency-based target. Let's see this question in action with the following nonproficiency-based target: *I can determine models using key features.*

- **Possible question:** How are students going to show you they know this? (Moss & Brookhart, 2012)

- **Possible answers:** Students will demonstrate this by creating an appropriate model, in all situations and including justification for key features.

- **Resulting proficiency-based target:** Using key features, determine the most appropriate model for a specific mathematical situation.

Sometimes it is hard for teachers to fully describe their expectations, but it can be easier to simply throw out one or two adjectives or words at a time that describe the process a student is going through while learning. By asking a colleague to simply speak about how the student would show proficiency, you will get a variety of terms, adjectives, and ideas that can be used to create a proficiency-based target.

What Does the End Product Look Like?

By asking teachers to visualize what the end product looks like and describe it, the language that they produce is often representative of a proficiency-based target. Let's see this question in action with the following nonproficiency-based target: *I can determine models using key features.*

- **Possible question:** Describe the ideal student answer.

- **Possible answers:** They have to include the appropriate model, they must do it in all situations, and they have to provide justification for key features, not just list them.

- **Resulting proficiency-based target:** Using key features, determine the most appropriate model for a specific mathematical situation.

With teachers focused on lesson planning and best practice, it is difficult for them to articulate what they ideally want from students. With changing textbooks, rapidly evolving technology, and overdeveloped curricula, teachers may be far removed from their ideal expectation of students. This question helps teachers articulate what the end product looks like and ultimately discover their learning target.

What Is the Purpose of This Work?

Asking teachers to describe the purpose of the work within the context of learning, it will begin to tease out proficiency language. Let's see this question in action with the following nonproficiency-based target: *I can determine models using key features.*

- **Possible question:** Why are students doing this work?

- **Possible answers:** Students are doing this work to learn key features and how to find accurate models but also to tell me why or why not they used a key feature.

- **Resulting proficiency-based target:** Using key features, determine the most appropriate model for a specific mathematical situation.

By asking teachers to describe purpose, a more proficiency-centered conversation can blossom resulting in flexible language that can be used to create proficiency-based targets.

How Will I Measure This Work?

Asking teachers how they will measure the work will tease out language that describes through what means a student will demonstrate emerging skill or knowledge (Moss & Brookhart, 2012). Examples of this language are *in writing, in a text, with supporting details*, and so on. This language helps teachers clarify what a proficiency-based target looks like in their mind's eye. Let's see this question in action with the following nonproficiency-based target: *I can determine models using key features.*

- **Possible question:** How are students expected to engage with this target?

- **Possible answers:** I am going to give them a bunch of different models, and they have to figure out which is the best model based on the key features that are shown. They also have to write why it is the best model.

- **Resulting proficiency-based target:** Using key features, determine and completely label the most appropriate model for a specific mathematical situation.

While we know that there is not a lot of *eduspeak* in these questions, we have found that teachers understand them at a gut level, and they have been helpful to teachers as they focus on developing proficiency-based learning targets. We should note that teachers generally have their expectations embedded in their assessments, so we must tease them out. Asking them to describe the assessment draws out that hidden language of proficiency and allows them to hear the proficiency-based target beginning to form.

Ensuring Targets Are Proficiency Based

Even after creating a target, it may still not be entirely proficiency based. To ensure that the target is proficiency based, teams and teachers can ask themselves the following questions when reviewing newly created learning targets.

- Does the learning target contain quantitative language?

- Does the learning target contain negative language?

- Does the learning target have context?

These ensure that the target will live effectively within curriculum, instruction, and assessment.

Does the Learning Target Contain Quantitative Language?

Quantitative language is any numerical wording that forces the learner to perceive that proficiency is achieved by crossing some threshold of accumulation or *amount*. Quantitative language is *detrimental* to the assessment process as it forces an outcomes-based mindset in the student. This mindset stifles growth and permits shallow learning. When exposed to quantitative language, students interpret proficiency to mean "the number of times that I . . ." or "the number of pieces I include or find in . . ."

Examples of quantitative targets include the following.

- I can identify *three out of five main ideas* from a text.

- I can identify the main idea from a text a *majority* of the time.

- I can identify *some* of the main ideas from a text.

Student learning doesn't blossom with quantitative targets because all students have to do is hit a certain amount in order to show mastery in the expectation.

Does the Learning Target Contain Negative Language?

This seems pretty straightforward *not* to include in targets but is actually difficult to avoid. When describing a performance, it is far too easy to state what a student *didn't* include. As we stated in chapter 1, targets represent an expectation of proficiency. These expectations include language of success, not language of deficiency. The purpose of proficiency-based targets is to explain what a student can do, and including negative language clouds that purpose.

Examples of targets that include negative language are as follows.

- I can identify the main idea from a text with *minimal error*.

- I can identify the main idea from a text *without* details.

- I can identify the main idea from a text with a *pattern of error*.

With negative language, a target loses its power to provide adequate and effective feedback. If teachers focus on deficiency, students are less likely to accept the feedback than if teachers were to use more proficiency-based language in their target.

Does the Learning Target Have Context?

Writing targets to include a proficiency expectation is a difficult task, much harder than one would think. This difficulty mainly stems from teachers attempting to create targets without context that frames how the target relates to each level of learning. Similar to what Marzano (2003) outlines as the different levels of curriculum, learning has levels as well, and with each level there is a specific purpose.

In the first part of our team's story, we saw Bruce lead the team through what is referred to as the *curricular hierarchy*, a template for teachers to outline the levels of learning. This curricular hierarchy has four levels and guides teachers in the development of effective proficiency-based targets. Without creating this hierarchy first, proficiency-based targets will be difficult to develop. The framework is presented in table 2.1.

Table 2.1: The Four Levels of the Proficiency-Based Assessment Curricular Hierarchy

Hierarchy Level	Learning Level Purpose	Core Questions
1	Big Idea (Provides Context)	Why are we doing all of this? What does everything relate to?
2	Skills Being Assessed (Performed, Assessed, Observed)	What am I asking you to do?
3	How Well a Student Must Demonstrate Skills (Proficiency Expectation)	What is my expectation of you?
4	Conditions for Success (Provided Resources or Content)	What are the resources, prerequisite skills, tools, or fundamental components required to meet the expectation?

Answering the core questions from table 2.1 will help collaborative teams better understand each level of learning, what they want students to learn, how they expect them to improve, and what mastery of the learning target will ultimately look like.

After all these checks and balances, a team should be in a great spot to produce a full proficiency-based target in an accurate learning context. A finished proficiency-based target *with the full contextual hierarchy* would appear something like the following.

1. Mathematical reasoning

2. Determining models

3. Using key features, determine the appropriate model for a specific mathematical situation.

4. Common ratio, y-intercept, and so on

Establishing quality proficiency-based targets in an accurate context is the most essential step to quality instructional and assessment experiences. Once the context has been established, gradations can be determined.

Commitment 2: Creating Learning Gradations

Although terrific educators like Susan Brookhart have been pointing the way, their work is often misinterpreted and misapplied, and learning targets are often written at the knowledge level as absolutes of either knowing or not knowing, where there is no middle range, no transition, and no "almost there." But, as we have stated, learning involves transition, and learning targets need to allow for it to occur.

As the team discussed in the story, gradations represent four stages of proficiency. Following is a more in-depth explanation of each stage (Guskey & Jung, 2013; Marzano, 2010; Moss & Brookhart, 2012).

4   **Exceeds expectations:** Students in this category consistently and substantially exceed requirements and perform at maximum levels of effectiveness.

3   **Meets expectations:** Students in this category consistently meet requirements of the target and perform in a fully expected and reliable manner.

2   **Approaching expectations:** Students in this category may inconsistently meet established targets and standards or may regularly fail to meet one or more of the established targets.

1   **Emerging understanding:** Students in this category may demonstrate basic levels of comprehension or skill development. Students may show growth that is disconnected from the target, or there is no pattern to their successes with the targets. Students regularly fail to meet one or more of the established targets.

Remember the initial gradation from the team's story?

4—I can analyze the causes of World War I.

3—I can explain the causes of World War I.

2—I can define the causes of World War I.

1—I can identify the causes of World War I.

On the surface, this gradation may appear effective, but it actually has a major flaw. It's incredibly important to note that targets are not effective unless the verb remains consistent throughout each gradation of learning. In the example in the team story earlier in this chapter, the verb changes in each gradation (which they will come to realize is problematic as they move through subsequent phases of their journey). This example appears to be focusing on the idea of *explaining*—the verb in the stage 3 gradation (the target gradation). On closer inspection, though, each gradation is asking the student to complete a *different task*!

Identifying different tasks within a set of gradations makes everything else that we do in the classroom that much more difficult—especially assessment. While each individual level of the scale may suggest viable methods of assessment, the gradations do not represent any single assessment, and a single assessment cannot identify a student's proficiency on a scale that represents four distinct skills. We would need four different assessments for this one scale! Using a target that is based on four different verbs (actions) may cause misguided lessons and stagnate learning.

Let's look at an accurate set of gradations from a world language course.

4—Independently create an appropriate spoken message in unfamiliar and unstructured situations.

3—Independently create an appropriate spoken message in familiar and unstructured situations.

2—Independently create an appropriate spoken message in familiar and structured situations.

1—Independently attempt to create an appropriate spoken message in familiar and structured situations.

Notice that in this example the verb or action is steady throughout all four levels. To study this concept further, let's look at an effective gradation and an ineffective gradation in a context we can all visualize: a baby learning to walk (table 2.2, page 58).

As we use these gradations to assess our baby's progress, our assessment of walking should never involve the other skills of crawling and running—those are, of course, different skills. Our assessment should begin by focusing on walking and remain focused on walking. In the left column, the verb is changing, causing what we would call a disjointed assessment structure. Ask yourself this question while looking at the left column: "What is the expectation here? Is it to run? To walk? To crawl?"

Table 2.2: Proficiency Scale Comparison

Gradation	Incorrect Scale	Proficiency-Based Scale
1	The baby can sit up.	The baby can walk with the aid of a walker.
2	The baby can crawl.	The baby can walk while holding mom's hand.
3	The baby can walk.	The baby can walk with no outside supports.
4	The baby can run.	The baby can walk over difficult terrain while barefoot.

In the right column, the expectation is clearly walking as it doesn't change between the levels. The only language that changes is the measurability of the target. The baby may be able to walk holding mom's hand but not by him- or herself. With the expectation focus held on walking—the *action*—and a change in the measurable or proficient language of the target, the target becomes clearer and more pedagogically valuable.

Teachers and teams can effectively create proficiency-based learning gradations by following these two simple tips.

1. **Represent success:** Make each level of the gradation a successful learning space for students. In other words, don't say, "At this level, the student can't do the skill or can't do it consistently." This would be an example of negative language, which we want to avoid. Rather, each level should represent where a student can and will be successful.

    4—*Use maps of different scales* to describe locations of *different* cultural and environmental characteristics.

    3—*Use maps of different scales* to describe the locations of *similar* cultural and environmental characteristics.

    2—*Use maps of same scale* to describe the locations of *similar* cultural and environmental characteristics.

    1—*Use a map* to describe the locations of *similar* cultural and environmental characteristics.

2. **Include flexible language:** Instead of listing all content pieces individually as targets, list them with flexible language. For example, instead of a target saying, "Students can analyze the Battle of the Bulge" or "Students can analyze the time line of D-Day," the target should state, "Students can analyze historical events in a structured context." Following is an example of gradations for this concept in a fifth-grade mathematics target.

> 4—I can accurately write and interpret numerical expressions in unfamiliar situations.
>
> 3—I can accurately write and interpret numerical expressions in familiar situations.
>
> 2—I can appropriately write and interpret numerical expressions in familiar situations.
>
> 1—I can attempt to write and interpret numerical expressions in familiar situations.

A proficiency-based gradation of learning creates not only a learning pathway for students to follow but also a guide for quality assessment, effective instruction, and sound curriculum for teachers.

Commitment 3: Using Targets Effectively in Instruction

One thing that we know for certain is that although many teachers have written and produced thousands of learning targets, not all of them make it fully into the instructional practice of teachers and the learning experience of students. In our observation of teachers, most learning targets remain stagnant, imprisoned on review worksheets, daily agendas, rubrics, and exams and quizzes—simply communicating to the student that an assessment is *concerning* the target.

During this stage of team learning, some teachers do not yet see that there *is* a correlation between a well-written and developed proficiency-based learning target and quality teaching and learning (Marzano, 2006). It is important for teachers to see the distinction between supporting content and skills (the seemingly infinite amount of facts and absolute skills that one must learn) and the target (or the "how well" language of an assessment).

How to Maintain a Target's Instructional Importance

An observer can easily spot a lack of proficiency-based targets in many classrooms by listening carefully to the questions that are posed during the lesson. For example, the presence of questions that are posed to *check* student understanding typically indicates a lack of proficiency-based targets (Danielson, 2007). To keep proficiency-based targets at the center of learning, the lesson and all dialogue within must focus on the language of the target at all times. Consider how the following teacher, Ms. Apple, attempted to maintain a proficiency focus on the target *Cite strong and thorough textual evidence to support analysis of inferences drawn from the text* in a language arts class while studying *Hamlet*. There are three foci that a proficiency-based target needs: (1) student focus, (2) teacher focus, and (3) lesson focus.

1. **Student focus:** Ms. Apple relates all student actions and reactions to the proficiency language of the target. For example, if a student answers a question, Ms. Apple might respond with "Yes . . . and we see that here in the target." Or, if a student is producing work, Ms. Apple might suggest, "Remember to be proficient and add more evidence in your work that supports your inference that the main character does not like others' opinions."

2. **Teacher focus:** Ms. Apple also varies the type of questioning and activities; however, she makes sure that all students have an observable relation to the proficiency language of the target. In the classroom, teachers must relate all questioning to the proficiency-based targets. In this lesson, Ms. Apple may ask students, "Do you have enough evidence to make a strong case for that inference?" She creates activities that allow students to develop citing skills and manipulate textual evidence.

   Teachers must intentionally plan based on the proficiency aspects of the target rather than try to create a plan that fits into a theme or a unit that has been structured by a textbook.

3. **Lesson focus:** By using the gradation, Ms. Apple can tailor the activities, task, assessment, or even dialogue to each individual student (Moss & Brookhart, 2012). The full gradation of this lesson is as follows.

   4—Cite strong and thorough textual evidence to support insightful analysis of inferences drawn from the text.

   3—Cite strong and thorough textual evidence to support analysis of inferences drawn from the text.

   2—Cite strong textual evidence to support analysis of inferences drawn from the text.

   1—Cite textual evidence to support analysis of inferences drawn from the text.

By maintaining these three foci, teachers like Ms. Apple can create a high sense of connectedness between learners and the intended learning. This enables them to assess and instruct their students simultaneously, all the while keeping the focus of their lessons squarely on the proficiency-based target.

How to Mobilize a Target in Instruction

By *mobilize*, we mean that the target is made an active learning tool for the student. Students hear far too often "Today, students, we will be learning about [target]," and that is the extent of the target's instructional life! By mobilizing the target to be active in the learning process, students can now use it to reflect, organize their thoughts, review their own work and their peers', and ultimately self-assess. This mobilization makes the student see the target as the center of the learning process.

We are the first to admit that it can be exhausting to effectively instruct with the proficiency-based target if not done properly. To compensate for this, lessons tend to be based on a systematic scaffolding of content and skills to ensure learning. While we agree with the concept of scaffolding in general, we have specific problems with how scaffolding actually occurs in many classrooms. In many cases, the scaffolding of lessons has removed the teacher's need for proficiency awareness by making instruction more linear and methodical. A teacher can be excused from focusing on a proficiency-based learning target because the scaffolded lesson plan calls the teacher to simply execute each segment of the lesson in a linear time line—assuming that doing so will allow each student to master the intended target, due to the easily digestible nature of each small scaffolded segment.

We know that this doesn't always work. By incorporating a proficiency-based learning target into our instructional practice, we make it much more likely that students will achieve the intended level of mastery as we have them constantly reflect on how well they are performing. We can't guarantee that we can get all students to assess their own level of understanding at all times, but we can make it much more likely if we can communicate our own expectation of proficiency and have the student frequently tell us and themselves how they are doing. There are several ways we can do this.

Constantly Connect Learning to the Proficiency-Based Target

As teachers, it is important that we make regular statements about what the expected proficiency is. Whenever there is an opportunity to connect what a student says or does to the target's proficiency expectation, do so. An example would be when a teacher is walking around to view student work and says, "I like what you are doing here with [language of the target]" or "I see what you are trying to do here, so make sure [language of the target] is more evident."

Let's look at this target from a world language classroom: *I can create original oral meaning that is clear and organized and elaborates with supporting details in simple context.* A teacher in this world language classroom can make the target come alive by saying, "I am not sure what you are trying to say here. Remember clarity is important" or "Your thoughts have detail, but I would ask that you speak about [general interests] before [specific hobby] to make more sense."

Greet Students With the Proficiency-Based Target

Give students the learning layout prior to each lesson and explain how it relates to the targeted expectation. An example would be when a teacher says, "The tasks that we will be engaging in today are all connected to [language of the target]" or "What I am looking for in regard to [language of the target] is . . ."

With the target *I can create original oral meaning that is clear and organized and elaborates with supporting details in simple context,* a teacher could say, "Remember, to be original means to include personal stories or experiences, maybe something that happened at your swim meet this weekend . . ." or "Class, this dialogue is about school sports, something you know well. If you want to demonstrate something more advanced, I need you to produce original meaning with a more advanced topic such as school bullying. Either way is fine, but I expect simple context only."

Make the Proficiency-Based Target Relatable

Whenever a student offers up evidence, thinking, or a reaction that is related to the target, grab it and teach with it. An example of this would be when a teacher says, "That is right, Johnny. That information is what we are looking for here in [language of the target]" or "What that group just presented is what we mean by [language of the target]."

With the target *I can create original oral meaning that is clear and organized and elaborates with supporting details in simple context,* a teacher can make the target relatable by saying, "That is one of the major ways to elaborate details. Thanks, Group A. We need to remember [Group A's insight]" or "Class, let me bring up something Jonny just said. He said that originality can be expressed in speaking by [strategy for finding authentic voice]."

Reflect on the Proficiency-Based Target

The importance of reflection is undeniable in today's classrooms, and as proficiency-based assessment states, effective reflection needs to involve a quality target. A student needs to self-reflect during the lesson, and teachers can use the target as a mirror to facilitate that reflection.

An example of making a target a mirror would be when a teacher asks the students, "Can you see your work in the [language of the target] yet?" or "What thinking may go into [language of the target]?"

With the target *I can create original oral meaning that is clear and organized and elaborates with supporting details in simple context*, creating this mirror would look like this: "Susie, are you certain that all your details elaborate on the context of school sports?" or "Remember, class, look at your dialogue. Does it flow logically from one detail to the next about school sports?"

Commitment 4: Developing Assessment Literacy

Our daily work in schools reflects a dynamic interplay among curriculum, instruction, and assessment. When we hear teachers and administrators discuss their work, we often hear that they feel very comfortable writing curriculum or that they have a deep understanding of their content. We love hearing conversations about the powerful lessons that they are developing for students. Interestingly enough, not one of us has ever heard a teacher proclaim, "I am an assessment expert!"

Assessment is the one part of our craft that tends to get the most attention with the least amount of scrutiny (Ainsworth & Viegut, 2006). In other words, there are educators who are constantly creating and revising assessments and rubrics without ever taking the time to consider how effective they are in promoting learning. The two biggest issues with traditional assessment are that it doesn't accommodate student growth and it doesn't capture student thought patterns (Bailey & Jakicic, 2012).

Accommodating Student Growth

To accommodate growth, assessments must align first and foremost with the learning gradation. If the targeted gradation is in alignment with the assessment, then it is more likely that students are being assessed at *all* levels of competency and proficiency. As a result, more meaningful evidence is produced, and teachers can use it to make an accurate evaluation of their students (Marzano, 2009).

Let's look at our language arts target gradation from Ms. Apple's class again.

4—Cite strong and thorough textual evidence to support insightful analysis of inferences drawn from the text.

3—Cite strong and thorough textual evidence to support analysis of inferences drawn from the text.

2—Cite strong textual evidence to support analysis of inferences drawn from the text.

1—Cite textual evidence to support analysis of inferences drawn from the text.

Most traditional assessments for this gradation would only create questions for stage 3, maybe, for example, as an exam of fifty questions all centered on citing evidence. However, for assessment to accurately accommodate growth, it must also include questions that focus on stages 4 and 2 of the gradation. This would allow for sections that prompt the students to provide insight into their citations (stage 4) and also include sections that ask for simple citations of evidence (stages 2 and 3). By gauging other stages of the gradation, an assessment now has the ability to challenge students to not only develop an intended proficiency but also show them where they are growing.

Capturing Student Thought Patterns

Most traditional quizzes and tests assess students on whether they have mastered specific outcomes, only later asking students to think about their answers. We believe that it is more important that assessments focus on the reactions and thought patterns of students *as* they are answering questions (Schoemaker, 2011). If teachers can capture the in-assessment thinking, then they will have a better shot at creating an accurate picture of their students' learning.

Let's look at a health class target.

4—I can appropriately analyze influences on my well-being in a variety of unfamiliar contexts.

3—I can accurately analyze influences on my well-being in a variety of familiar contexts.

2—I can appropriately analyze influences on my well-being in a variety of familiar contexts.

1—I can attempt to analyze influences on my well-being in a variety of familiar contexts.

Assessments that capture thinking contain questions such as "How would you describe the process of solving this problem?" or "As you worked through the last three problems, what strategies did you use the most to solve them?" These questions focus learners away from outcomes and into an analysis of their own thought.

Notice that these are starkly different from questions like "How did you feel about the last answer: sure, unsure, or undecided?" or "Give your answer and explain why you chose that answer," which place importance on finding outcomes or reflecting on how one feels about an outcome (Stiggins, Arter, Chappuis, & Chappuis, 2004).

Avoiding Assessment Pitfalls

In his article "The Unfulfilled Promise of Classroom Assessment," Rick Stiggins (2001b) argues that the major issues that occur with assessment are low levels of assessment literacy among teachers and administration, inaccurate assessment of the achievement of students, ineffective feedback to students about their achievement, and the failure of students to reach their full potential. Teachers and collaborative teams can perform what we like to call an *assessment MRI* to measure the effectiveness of an assessment by checking for the following indicators.

- **The assessment is ambiguous:** Ambiguous assessments are assessments that are either too simplistic or too complex in structure. This means the tasks used to capture student learning are either too easy or so complicated that students don't understand how to navigate a particular segment of the assessment.

- **The assessment is imbalanced:** Imbalanced means the assessment is based on one level of knowledge (Marzano, 2009). Assessments must represent the gradation of learning, as we described previously, by dedicating segments of the assessment to each level of the learning target gradation.

- **The assessment suffers from DRIP syndrome:** *DRIP* stands for data rich, information poor. Assessments that suffer from DRIP syndrome are assessments that produce large amounts of student evidence that yield little insight into how the student is performing. These assessments may be long and laborious as the creators of these assessments confuse frequency for proficiency. With so much data, teachers struggle to uncover clear evidence of student proficiency from the assessment, and students can't tell if they did well or not (DuFour, DuFour, Eaker, & Karhanek, 2004).

- **The assessment is uncommon:** For assessments to drive instructional change, a team of teachers must be able to collaboratively evaluate their data. An uncommon assessment means the assessment is not the same among all team members, causing limited collaboration and data confusion.

- **All assessments are product based:** Product-based assessments have the potential to force outcomes-based learning. This type of assessment is used for verification of learning instead of supporting learning. Product-based assessments that regularly exist in product-based form are entrance and exit slips, postassessment reflective activities, review packets, and summative experiences, to name a few.

Building Proficiency-Based Assessment Literacy

Proficiency-based assessments should vary based on the needs of the student at any given point in the unit (Danielson, 2007). Ideally, these assessments should be seamlessly integrated with the instruction such that the students might not even recognize the assessment event (Wiliam, 2011). To achieve a seamless assessment environment, teachers need to be literate in the following types of assessment and employ them in their instruction.

- **Declarative assessment:** Assessing the "what" knowledge

- **Conditional assessment:** Assessing the "why" knowledge

- **Procedural assessment:** Assessing the "how" knowledge

- **Application assessment:** Assessing use of flexible knowledge in all contexts

- **Problem-solving assessment:** Assessing the use of knowledge or skills to engage an issue or problem

- **Critical-thinking assessment:** Assessing the evaluation of concepts

- **Communication assessment:** Assessing the communication skill of understanding

- **Synthesis assessment:** Assessing the connections made by the learner of concepts, processes, and skills (Badders, 2000)

But how does a teacher know which type of assessment to build and when to use it? Here we are informed by one of the basic principles of architecture and design— form follows function. Ultimately, the learning target is the guide that dictates which assessment type a teacher must choose (Wiggins & McTighe, 2005). This highlights the important fact that proficiency-based gradations are not only our instructional guide but our map to discover a more quality assessment experience.

Key Points

Following are key points from the chapter that readers should review to ensure they have a firm grasp on the content.

- The team and each teacher must be able to identify the benefits of proficiency-based assessment over traditional outcomes-based assessment. They should have a strong understanding as to why proficiency-based assessment is important to student growth.

- All team members must know how to compose effective learning targets. This will ensure that the development of the work is focused on student learning, that it will hold students to high expectations, and that your team will invest in a shared agreement around what all students should be able to know, understand, and do.

- Each target must be clearly scaled and gradations of learning clearly articulated.

- A team can always return to the preparation phase to learn more, develop its depth of understanding, or just review understanding.

Chapter 3

Incubation

At this point in our team's journey—after developing a sturdy foundation during the preparation phase—our team now enters the incubation phase. You might think about the incubation phase as a period of time when the idea is under construction, connections are being made, and ideas and considerations start to really come to mind and are listed as possibilities. Some find it useful to brainstorm during this phase. Some see it as a time for developing idea generation and questioning. It is similar to all of those activities, but incubation strives to go a bit deeper. During this phase, individuals and teams are making deeper sense of the possibility of a change and how it might integrate logically and significantly with the work of the individual or team. It marks the period when ideas percolate—both good and bad ideas. It is a thinking period of time, a chance for individuals to make sense of the resources and ideas from the preparation phase. This is the time when individuals and teams allow for ideas to bounce around; they consider, reconsider, question, mull over, and discuss. During this phase, individuals and teams are making sense of the new learning—thoughts might be simple in their construction or wildly divergent in their possibility. The individual or the team as a whole is trying to put shape around understanding and how to apply it.

Because it specifically requires us to re-envision how we can work with assessment differently—more effectively—the incubation phase is a significant step for any individual or team. This will take some time. Remember, in asking teachers to rethink assessment, you are asking them to reconceive a lifetime of practices. Don't rush. This phase takes time, a thoughtful approach, and a lot of support. Individuals and teams struggle during this phase. They may need clarification, or they may need to dip back into the preparation phase and revisit research. They might need to reread, collect data, or seek out other expertise for guidance. They will likely need more time to process their thinking. As the incubation phase continues, individuals and teams will begin to connect the dots; teams will connect more authentically to the *why* behind the work, they will begin to identify possibilities for how the work can better teaching and learning, and they will think of ways to integrate the change for valuable purposes. Again, the focus is on developing the potential of every student.

Following are three key points to remember during the incubation phase.

1. Authentic dialogue is key. Brainstorming and possibility thinking fuel the incubation phase.

2. Questioning and challenging one another are helpful activities as teams work to make contributions and add their expertise. If questioning or confusion continues, this might reveal a lack of clarity or the need to return to the preparation phase.

3. Leadership is highly communicative and interactive. Teams need to help one another to have their questions and concerns addressed quickly. When teams ask questions, those questions are legitimate; however, they need clear responses that make sense and are tied to a rationale for effective change.

As you read the story in this chapter about our team's experience in the incubation stage, notice how the characters interact with the new learning and percolate ideas about assessment and how ideas are generated in a supportive, sense-making discussion space. Consider the following questions as you read regarding the incubation of proficiency-based assessment ideas.

- In what ways does the team begin to see how targets interact with assessments, how targets interact with instruction, and how assessments interact with instruction?

- What questions are the teachers asking while they are brainstorming around proficiency-based assessment? Are they coming up with multiple ways in which proficiency-based assessment works well for their specific students' learning?

- Is the leadership around proficiency-based assessment ensuring the team is maintaining fidelity, or are they drifting? Does the team need more supportive preparation?

Our Team's Story

Walking back from a class one day, Bruce noted that there was something missing from his lesson. He felt like nothing was getting through to students, no matter what he tried. His assessment process felt clunky and sometimes unmanageable with the amount of formative assessments he was giving his students. He wondered about the process of creating proficiency gradations he was just starting to understand. He thought it would take a lot of time and a lot of decisions about what his students' learning really looked like and sounded like.

Bruce felt that he had exhausted almost all the methods of having students interact with the gradations of learning. It simply seemed superficial—like assessment was only about checking for learning each and every day. Bruce decided he needed to learn more about the work of scaling targets so that he could really understand the impact it could have on his students, and he had questions about the role of indicators. He spent the next several weeks researching and discussing these questions with his colleagues and administrators. What Bruce learned during those few weeks was an all-important, often-overlooked piece of the assessment puzzle.

When the time came for the next team meeting, Bruce felt that he had a stronger grasp on how to lead his team through the incubation phase—the stage of pondering and reshaping and thinking and questioning. As his teammates entered the meeting, Bruce was not surprised when he heard that they held the same questions about scaling targets he had. Each team member was struggling with the same question: "There has to be more to these targets than simply progressions, doesn't there? Surely there is something more to this process!"

Vaughn opened up the meeting by stating that she was exhausted. "I am constantly asking my students at the end of the class where they are on the scale with little payoff," she says. "I am not sure what the scale is giving us except a new way to do a rubric."

Morrison nodded in agreement and said, "These scales are no better than the rubrics I've given in the past."

Likewise, Britney stated that she struggled to see the value in the gradation as it "simply feels like scaffolding practice the team has always done."

On the other hand, Joni felt a bit more optimistic. She told the team she felt like her lessons were "far more organized and purposeful." Joni noted that she was working to notice how the curriculum was showing up in the assessment and how her instruction was interlocked, working backward from the assessment. She commented, "My lessons are more unified and directly connected to what our assessment is asking of them."

Bruce admitted that he felt that the gradations were not moving the class as much as he had hoped. He said, "I felt that targeted gradations remained isolated and distinct components of my lessons instead of integrated."

Frustrated, Morrison said, "I thought this would happen. So what do we do now? I don't want to put in any more work unless it's going somewhere."

Bruce, feeling the team pulling away from the strides it made during the first meeting, decided it was a good time to bring up his realization from the last few weeks.

Bruce jumped in, "After a few weeks of implementing these gradations, I felt the same way as all of you. At first, it felt like a great new tool, but then it became a simple rubric or a superficial reflection tool without a purpose. I was using it as a quick check at the end of the lesson."

Bruce continued, "Targets are essential to assessment, but when they do not meet the *three-target test*, they will never merge completely with assessment. Instead, the target will remain an unsatisfying isolated element of your class. There are three requirements to creating effective targets. Number one is all targets must contain a proficiency expectation. Number two is all targets must be measurable. And number three is all targets must be on a gradation of *one* type of thinking or skill. Targets, which are the linchpin of the assessment process, must be measurable and proficient—a gradation of one type of thinking or skill. Since most targets struggle to pass the three-target test, assessments serve only as products."

There was a long pause, and after several moments of silence, Joni, sensing the rest of the team was confused, interjected, "So what does that mean? The assessment process breaks down if we don't have quality targets based on proficiency?"

Bruce said quickly, "Yes. Joni, I was wondering the same thing. I was worried that our assessments aren't as good as we think they are. And that is what I discovered." He continued, "Assessment is not what we think it is. It is not a product. Having assessments that are process based can shorten students' reaction time to feedback, can increase opportunities for reflection, and can now be integrated into instruction. In order to create effective targets, we must use the target test. If we can do that, we will be better able to communicate what skills we want to see from our students."

Britney replied, "We already have a target test. We need to be specific, we need to put it in student-friendly language, and it must contain a depth of knowledge verb on the gradation."

Bruce shook his head. "That is what I thought," he said, "but several colleagues helped me and clarified that all targets must satisfy these three requirements to successfully become part of the assessment process."

The room was silent as everyone processed the information. Bruce knew that the incubation phase would be filled with long pauses and pondering because it really challenges new learning and information and that pushback is natural and challenging questions should emerge. He realized that the role of leadership is to keep the dialogue focused and connected to the characteristics of change that the team is striving to implement.

After a few minutes of silence, Vaughn asked, "So how do we do this target test then?"

Bruce, sensing some interest, decided to begin. He led his team through some exercises. He started with this: "The first question we ask is, 'Does the target have a proficiency expectation?'"

Morrison asked, "What is a proficiency expectation?"

Joni reminded everyone, "Remember, proficiency-based assessment refers to it as a state of competency that acts as a learning outcome."

Morrison added, "So . . ."

Bruce responded, "What it means is that our expectation of competency or mastery of the skill is the targeted outcome, not the verb. Essentially it is not what students can do, but more of how well they can do it."

This seemed to puzzle the group more, so Bruce worked to clarify. "This is what I learned," he said. "Proficiency language is difficult to find and is almost absent from targets that are presented to students. The absence of proficiency language forces instruction into an absorption model instead of a reflective model, but we will get to that later."

Bruce decided to switch gears and said, "Let's look at our target. *Students will be able to explain the causes of World War I.* Most teachers would argue that this target is clear, specific, and attainable. However, this target does not contain any language of proficiency or a state of expected competency. By using the proficiency-based assessment lens, a teacher would better communicate to students with the following revision: *Students will be able to effectively explain the main political, economic, and social causes of World War I.* With this simple addition of *effectively* and *main*, the students now have a clearer picture of the 'how well' or how competent they must be in the proposed skill, concept, or performance."

Again some team members paused. They were all focused on the new information just presented.

Britney spoke up. "So that's it? Just add in those words?"

Bruce responded, "Yes, that is what proficiency-based assessment is telling us."

Joni, usually on board with most ideas, asked, "But it's so vague, so how does it help?"

Bruce explained, "These words are a pedagogical mechanism that builds two purposes: for the teacher (1) to clearly articulate the desired state of competency and (2) to act as a portal for students to clarify competency expectations—thus opening up a student-teacher dialogue for any given outcome of any given lesson."

Morrison, starting to engage a bit more, added, "So how have we missed this language all this time? Why is it suddenly important?"

Bruce added, "It has always been important! But with so much going on within our teaching roles these days it is easy to miss integral aspects of initiatives like proficiency-based assessment. Most professional development presents the final product, and many aspects are simply glossed over or missed completely. In this case, it is the proficiency language that was overlooked."

Britney confirmed, "OK. So what I am hearing is that we need to add proficiency language to all targets before we scale?"

Bruce answered, "Yes. But we need to add measurability to the target as well."

Vaughn, sensing her inexperience was starting to cause confusion, stated, "OK. Can we look at the second requirement in the three-target test with the same target?"

Bruce said, "Sure." He started again: "While adding proficiency language to a target has an obvious value, it is still not enough. To effectively communicate with students, we must also make the targets measurable."

At this point, the team needed to revisit some of the basics. Bruce clarified the following four points.

1. Measurability is not the same as specificity. Measurable targets contain comparative and flexible language that clearly defines an expected state of proficiency.

2. When we effectively focus communication on proficiency, the same target, if it were measurable, might look like this: *Using examples from class, students will be able to effectively explain the main causes of World War I in a written analysis.*

3. By including *using examples from class* and *written analysis*, we have a clearer expectation that inherently draws student learning toward proficiency.

A teacher could also add something like this and be just as effective: *In a paragraph, students will be able to effectively explain the main causes of World War I in simple context.*

4. Creating measurable targets allows for a healthy foundation for formative assessment, clear and purposeful instruction, and accurate and meaningful reflection on the part of students. When we get clear about proficiency, we help students understand not only the learning expectation but also how well we expect them to know the content or skill.

After reviewing these four points, the team took another long pause. At this point, the energy started to pick up in the room.

Joni started to make some connections with the learning she gained during the preparation phase. She confidently added, "So I am starting to understand this. Let me see if I got this. Without this language, it is difficult for the students to see a learning finish line beyond that of mere short-term reproduction. Our learning targets must be written so that students can constantly assess their own cognitive or skill development against a stated proficiency expectation."

Bruce recognized that the work was starting to make clearer sense to the team. Team members like Joni were synthesizing the ideas into their own words, and they were articulating a sophistication of clarity.

Still questioning the idea, Morrison noted, "But how does this help scaling?"

Bruce added, "In an understanding of assessment that is proficiency based, targets must reflect multiple levels of proficiency—scales or gradations—and create reflective learning opportunities for students to experience as they adapt their understanding and skills while moving closer to proficiency. Let's look at the gradations we created for our World War I target during our last meeting." Bruce wrote the following on a chart.

4—I can analyze the causes of World War I.

3—I can explain the causes of World War I.

2—I can define the causes of World War I.

1—I can identify the causes of World War I.

He continued, "If we properly add proficiency, it would look something like the following." Bruce next wrote the following on the chart.

4—Using unique examples and opinions, students will be able to effectively explain the main causes of World War I in a written analysis.

3—Using examples from class, students will be able to effectively explain the main causes of World War I in a written analysis.

2—Using given definitions and terms, students will be able to effectively explain the main causes of World War I in a written analysis.

1—Using a text, students will be able to effectively explain the main causes of World War I in a written analysis.

Vaughn, recognizing the clarity, interjected, "Wow! There is a big difference with the revised target."

Bruce explained the difference: "By creating a gradation of learning that focuses in on one proficiency expectation for one student learning target, we move toward a more solid foundation in which students will be able to transfer knowledge and skills between levels of proficiency, develop a new understanding of what proficiency is, and quickly identify when they are or when they are not proficient."

Joni questioned, "So we shouldn't change the verb, but we should change the measurability and proficiency aspects of each target to create learning gradations?"

Bruce agreed and added, "Yes. The essential realization here is that targets are flexible dynamic instructional tools."

Joni suggested, "Let's do the test on all of our targets for the next unit and see what happens."

The other team members agreed and took out unit 2's targets, and they began to work. By the end of their meeting time, they had all of unit 2's targets tested and scaled.

Capitalizing on the team's progress, Bruce asked the team members to reflect on their new realizations.

Joni began, "Until now I never clearly understood how learning targets logically fit into our curriculum. I was never quite sure how to write them and embed them into instruction in a way that made sense to me. I feel like I see their purpose and their role in assessment. But they have to be properly written first."

Vaughn added, "I know. In the past, students had to memorize so many facts that multiple choice seemed like the only way to assess learning. I feel that by putting proficiency at the center of our work we will have fewer targets resulting in a variety of assessments instead of the one multiple-choice assessment approach we use now."

On that note, Bruce concluded the meeting and asked the team members to begin using their new proficiency-based targets in unit 2 and observing differences in their classroom, instruction, or assessment. The team members agreed that they were now working more correctly and clearly with the targets; however, they started to wonder how proficiency-based targets affect assessment, instruction, and reflection.

The Four Combinations Within Proficiency-Based Assessment

One of the great gifts in working within a collaborative culture is that the cycle of inquiry is never-ending. In our story, we see this as the team members are pushing themselves beyond the basic understanding of a learning target, and their conversation shifts to determine how well students are succeeding. When we shift our collaborative conversations to how well students are meeting a proficiency expectation, we can then begin to question the effectiveness of our instructional practices. During the incubation phase of team learning, it is easy for teams to get sidetracked as they begin to view their learning targets through a proficiency lens. With so many new thoughts generating, it is hard for teams to decipher how to move forward. This pedagogical blindness hinders teams from determining the best course of action through proficiency-based assessment.

Our experience has told us that teams develop this blindness during the incubation phase because they begin to observe how important it really is that the "how well" component is included in their learning targets. During this stage of dialogue and team learning, the pieces of proficiency-based learning targets start to come alive in teams' thinking, and the ideas of proficiency-based learning begin to emerge in the products they create and in their instruction. During the incubation phase, it is critical that teachers and teams continue to push their own and one another's thinking about what they hear, see, feel, and experience. During this phase, there are relationships between elements of proficiency-based assessment that teams must grapple with and think through, including the following four combinations.

1. Proficiency-based targets and instruction

2. Assessments and process

3. Assessment structure and frequency

4. Instruction and assessment

Combination 1: Proficiency-Based Targets and Instruction

As we work to bridge the assessment divide, one of the more persistent questions that continues to pop up is on the purpose of targets during instruction.

The common sentiment of teachers that we hear is "I know there is something more to learning targets, but I can't put my finger on it." Connie Moss and Susan Brookhart (2012) suggest that learning targets can be used as performance scales of competency and measurability. In this way, learning gradations can become pedagogical tools. When used during instruction, gradations set clear expectations for proficiency, create purpose for the instructional activities, make student-produced evidence malleable, and provide a script for our feedback (Marzano, 2010; Moss & Brookhart, 2012).

Why Gradations Are Instructionally Important

If a lack of awareness about the relationship between proficiency-based targets and instruction exists, a teacher will continuously view targets as disconnected from actual instruction. When this happens the pedagogical value of the target plummets. Some teachers assert, "I can't teach and report with targets. I have too much content to get through. I have to see if the students know this stuff and move on." In our experience, the full proficiency-based target is not used during instruction, and this is problematic. The following anecdote outlines this problem.

Let's take a look at a hypothetical discussion with a world history teacher who has the following learning target for a unit on the Renaissance: *Define the word* humanism.

A colleague asks the teacher how many possible ways a student could show him a quality definition, and he responds with the following.

- Synonym
- Bullet points
- Short definition
- Long definition
- Short definition with contextual evidence
- Long definition with contextual evidence
- Long definition with opinion
- Long definition with personal connection

The colleague asks, "And what is the assessment asking for?"

The teacher responds, "Long definition with contextual evidence."

"And how do you teach to the target?"

He answers with this.

- Synonym

- Bullet points

- Short definition

- Long definition

- Short definition with contextual evidence

- Long definition with contextual evidence

- Long definition with opinion

- Long definition with personal connection

The colleague then asks, "Why instruct using all the other stuff if it has no relation to your expectation?"

The teacher had never considered this before.

As we noted in chapter 2, the realization that proficiency-based learning targets can be pedagogical tools is an enlightening moment for teachers and teams. Seeing their proficiency-based target as instructional devices is a moment of discovery that can lead to a more focused and more purposeful lesson.

How a Proficiency-Based Target Enters Instruction

Consider the teacher in the preceding scenario we discussed. He clearly had targets properly conceptualized and valued them to the point of wanting to assess them. However, he was unsure of how to use the learning targets as an instruction tool. To support teachers and collaborative teams in their effort to make sense of the relationship between gradations and instructional practice, ask them to consider the following questions that help teachers prepare the learning environment for proficiency-based targets.

- How well does a student need to do this? (What does the proficiency we are measuring look like within our lesson of study?)

- What is the proficiency-based target's context?

- What will evidence of an expected proficiency look like?

- Can students retake an assessment or reperform?

- Do the activities that we plan center on the proficiency expectation that the gradations describe?

How Well Does a Student Need to Do This? (What Does the Proficiency We Are Measuring Look Like Within Our Lesson of Study?)

Teachers must understand their own desired level of competency before they can create lesson plans and teach students. Since finding your desired level of quality is quite difficult, these questions help focus the discussion on quality instead of action, content, or task.

Thinking through these questions allows proficiency language to surface and be brought to the forefront of any conversation about teaching and learning. Engaging in these questions invites teachers to use words and phrases such as *effectively, in writing, consistently, with substantial evidence, in simple context,* or *in familiar situations.*

Typically teachers discuss questions such as "What does this unit cover?" or "What does the assessment look like?" or "Do we have any good strategies to teach this content?" These questions produce collaborative conversations about specific content inclusion or exclusion, organization of themes, and the logistics of tasks and activities . . . none of which focuses on student proficiency.

What Is the Proficiency-Based Target's Context?

In the previous chapter, we discussed the curricular hierarchy. This hierarchy shows how a target relates to curriculum, instruction, and assessment. Following is an example of a curricular hierarchy with a completed proficiency-based target (the gradations at level 3) and full learning context.

1. Mathematical reasoning

2. Determining models

3. Determining the appropriate model for a specific situation that justifies using key features.

> 4—Using key features, determine the most appropriate model for all mathematical situations.
>
> 3—Using key features, determine the most appropriate model for a specific mathematical situation.
>
> 2—Using key features, determine a model for a specific mathematical situation.
>
> 1—When given key features, determine a model for a specific mathematical situation.

4. Common ratio, y-intercept, and so on

The purpose of this hierarchy is to ensure that teachers are thinking about and teaching with their gradation in the accurate context. The curricular hierarchy creates the instructional framework that a gradation needs to be meaningful in the classroom. Gradations without this curricular hierarchy supporting it have the potential to become disconnected from the learning process and lose value in the eyes of the learner.

What Will Evidence of an Expected Proficiency Look Like?

It is important for teachers and teams to build assessments that will allow students to show how well they can demonstrate the learning target, not just whether they can achieve a correct outcome. This means that assessments must collect the right evidence (Wiggins & McTighe, 2005). What we mean by *right* is the evidence that is connected to the proficiency language of the target.

In our mathematics target, *Using key features, determine the most appropriate model for a specific mathematical situation,* most current assessment practices would focus on the words *determine* and *model*. Unfortunately, these words are not the proficiency parts of the target. Using these words will lead to longer assessments that produce large amounts of evidence and summative experiences that create accountability for learning, but unfortunately, these words do not create the potential for an accurate determination of student success.

In our example, a more effective assessment would be created if the team based student assessment on the words and phrases *appropriate* and *justifies using key features*. These words are the proficient and measurable aspects of the target and must be used to create the assessment structure. In this case, evidence of achievement would come in one form, the "appropriate production of key features." By discussing what the evidence of proficiency might look like, teams can begin to create instructional experiences that are related to the proficiency-based target.

Can Students Retake an Assessment or Reperform?

To properly instruct with a proficiency-based target (which includes a set of four gradations), teams and teachers must begin to embrace the idea of reperformance. In our experience, teachers and administrators alike vary dramatically in their opinion of the purpose and feasibility of reperformance. While all this dissonance produces great conversation, the fact remains that reperforming tasks is something all people do every day and should be a practice that we embrace in education.

Reperformance is the vehicle that moves a student between the levels of the gradations of the proficiency-based target (Wiliam, 2011). Without reperformance, the student is unable to grow within the gradations of the proficiency-based targets, thus defaulting to the cram-and-slam short-term retention of facts and rote content. Therefore, we will make the argument again, as many experts have said before us, that without reperformance, only outcomes-based learning occurs.

Do the Activities That We Plan Center on the Proficiency Expectation That the Gradations Describe?

All activities and engagement in a lesson must connect to the proficiency and measurability language of the target. However, the truth is that most activities employed now are connected to the *verb* and *content theme* of the target.

In our mathematics example, *Using key features, determine the most appropriate model for a specific mathematical situation,* if a teacher is focused on the words *determine* and *situation,* then the instruction will be an unfocused variety of activities that ask students to determine models from situations. An observer would see activities that range from "what is a model," "what are key features," "determining," and "how to justify your model" activities.

But when we center all activities on the proficiency language of the gradation, we see a much different classroom landscape. In our example, if a teacher focused on the proficiency-based aspects of the target, *appropriate* and *justifies using key features,* an observer would see activities that are all related to how to justify your model.

Gradations are essential to focus the lesson on what is to be learned, guide our assessment of students, lead our reaction to student evidence, and mold our instructional actions. The combination of proficiency-based targets and instruction helps teachers begin to see their own expectation of quality as a pedagogical tool.

Teaching With a Proficiency-Based Target

Teaching with gradations only happens successfully when the following elements are present in the lesson.

- **Expectation of proficiency:** Teachers must present the expected level of competency at the beginning of each lesson. Teachers must ensure that each student understands the expectation before moving on in the lesson. Students must understand that it is the pathway to their learning, not just a communicative tool.

- **Formative assessments:** Teachers must engage students in the targeted gradation through a variety of formative assessments. The trick here is that teachers must possess a flexible knowledge of formative assessment so they can deploy many different assessments at any given time based on students' needs.

- **Performance windows:** Teachers must set expiration dates for targets. Not setting a date by which proficiency must be met causes logistical issues and concerns in growth. Engaging with a target must be contained to a specific amount of time. After that time is up, the teacher can decide whether a reperformance is necessary.

- **Reflection time:** Teachers must give adequate time to students to view their own work in the language of the gradation. Reflective spaces are critical to the learning process and must be valued by both teacher and student. This time is critical to receiving and acting on actionable feedback from an assessment experience.

By teaching through our proficiency-based targets, assessment conjoins with instruction; they become one and the same, creating highly effective learning environments. Teachers who master this concept dynamically change their lessons to meet each student's needs through differentiated experiences, and they also increase the likelihood that the grade they assign each student is more accurate.

Combination 2: Assessments and Process

During the incubation phase, teachers and collaborative teams are beginning to realize that their assessments are more than just products that verify student learning and achievement. We begin to see what Guskey and Jung (2013) mean when they suggest that, ideally, assessment is a process of evidence gathering, not a product that gathers evidence.

Finding the Purpose of the Assessment

As we work with teachers and curriculum teams all over North America, we ask them if they believe the following to be true: the purpose of assessment is not the verification of aptitude but, rather, the revealing of student thinking (Stiggins, 2008). Many educators we ask are stunned by the statement and wonder how an assessment can reveal thinking. The fact remains that we tend to think of assessment as a tool to gauge and pinpoint student understanding, not to monitor and support the student reflection process.

Some of us may have a vast knowledge of how to structure assessments but may not value how a student produces, clarifies, and employs thinking during an assessment. In proficiency-based assessment, this is the *purpose* of assessment: to support and validate the student reflection process. Moving toward an understanding of assessment as a reflective process encounters two distinct speed bumps that educators must overcome: (1) connecting assessments to proficiency-based targets and (2) connecting assessments to one another.

Speed Bump 1: Connecting Assessments to Proficiency-Based Targets

A simple yet effective method that we have found useful when creating proficiency-based assessments is the Target, Method, Match model that provides a template (see table 3.1, page 84) for teachers to create assessments by using their targeted gradations of learning (Stiggins et al., 2004).

Table 3.1: Target, Method, Match Chart

Learning Target	Type of Target	Assessment Method	Evidence

In this method, teachers or teams pick a gradation of their proficiency-based target, then select what type of assessment they want. Then, the teams record how they will gather evidence on the target. And finally the teams record how they will interpret the evidence. When this model is used, assessments are created that have the correct structure that will ultimately collect the right evidence of student learning.

Let's discuss each segment of this chart. First the learning target column describes the gradation of the proficiency-based target that a teacher intends to assess. Then, the type of target could be a knowledge target (targets that represent factual information), reasoning target (targets that represent reflective processes of students), skill target (targets that are performance or skill based), product target (targets based on creating a quality product), or disposition target (targets that refer to attitudes or motivations of students) (Stiggins et al., 2004). The assessment method column contains a description of the logistics of the assessment. And finally the evidence column is for recording the amount of evidence that is needed to make a judgment that a student is proficient.

When this practice is done correctly, we get nicely aligned assessment events to proficiency-based targets. Let's look at a few examples. The following example (figure 3.1) is a snapshot of a common assessment that was *not* developed with a Target, Method, Match model. The target that this reading assessment attempts to connect to is *I can read closely to determine what a text says explicitly* (it relates to CCSS .ELA-Literacy.CCRA.R.1; National Governors Association Center for Best Practices & Council of Chief State School Officers [NGA & CCSSO], 2010).

Short Answer: Answer the following questions.

1. Who were the "cowboys" that surrounded the wagon driver after he stopped for a drink?

2. Who is the "uncle" in paragraph twelve, and what is his connection to the group of cowboys in chapter 7?

3. In a few sentences, please explain the term "shop pigs" (line 86). Make sure you support your answer!

Figure 3.1: Sample assessment created without the Target, Method, Match model.

Notice that the questions seemingly assess content only and do not in any way reflect a proficiency-based target made of gradations. The directions simply ask the student to provide as much information as they remember. It will prove difficult to use the data produced by this assessment to determine where the student falls on the gradations of the target *I can read closely to determine what a text says explicitly.*

Now, let's look at a snapshot from another common assessment that is connected to a proficiency-based target and was developed using Target, Method, Match (see figure 3.2, page 86). The target that this assessment attempts to relate to is, again, *I can read closely to determine what a text says explicitly.*

Notice in this proficiency-based assessment that the questions are related to key reading strategies, there are bullets that clarify the proficiency and measurable language of the target, and there is also a proficiency-based rubric added for formative self-assessment. Without proper connection to proficiency-based targets, assessments may become unintentionally biased, ultimately unreliable, and contain no potential for reflection.

Speed Bump 2: Connecting Assessments to One Another

Some assessments are not focused on long-term thought patterns of learning but instead focus on short bursts of production (Schoemaker, 2011). As we have seen from various sources in recent years, using a higher frequency of formatives has proven to be more effective than larger summative experiences (Marzano, 2006). However, if they are not connected to one another, the formative assessments will feel disjointed with an unrelated purpose. In other words, formatives will feel to the students and teacher like a whole bunch of summative experiences. A teacher can overcome this speed bump by ensuring that all assessments are aligned to one another through the language of the proficiency-based target. To achieve this, teams can make a bubble chart and place the proficiency language of the target in the center and then brainstorm assessment methods that provide evidence toward that language (see figure 3.3, page 87).

This helps connect all assessments not only to the proficiency-based target but also to one another, illustrating a unified purpose.

If we are unable to move past these two speed bumps, we will continue to create an *outcomes-based learning environment* (Schoemaker, 2011). Our job then, in part, is to provide students with frequent opportunities to self-assess their own thinking and reasoning patterns as they engage in instructional and assessment experiences.

Please respond to the following questions.

1. Basic stated information: What did the thief take from the store owner?

2. Important details: What is the dog that Pete's uncle gave to him?

3. Stated relationships: How does Pete feel about the dog?

	4 Exceeds Mastery	3 Mastery	2 Approaching Mastery	1 Still Developing
Literal details	n/a	Completely determines what text says explicitly	Generally determines what text says explicitly	States details
Inferences	Accurately analyzes characters and plot using detailed and creative insight	Accurately analyzes characters and plot using detailed insight	Accurately analyzes characters and plot using limited insight	Generally analyzes characters and plot using limited insight
Author's message	Effectively analyzes a theme or central idea through detailed and creative insight	Effectively analyzes a theme or central idea through detailed insight	Effectively analyzes a theme or central idea through limited insight	Generally analyzes a theme or central idea through limited insight

Figure 3.2: Sample proficiency-based reading rubric for self-evaluation.

Independently create an appropriate spoken message in familiar and unstructured situations.

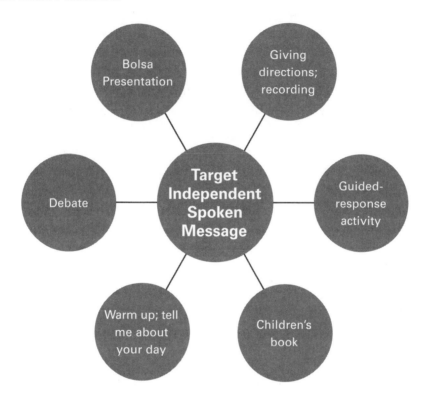

Figure 3.3: Example of bubble chart for brainstorming.

Moving From Product- to Proficiency-Based Assessments

Product-based assessment can be defined as an experience that does not occur during instruction, that is highly tangible, and that mimics a summative experience. Product-based assessments are more verification than transformation (Stiggins et al., 2004). While product-based assessments are not ineffective, they simply create outcomes-based learning environments through their summative nature. In other words, students see product-based assessments as attainment instead of growth (Stiggins et al., 2004).

We can take a huge step away from a product-based assessment culture and toward process-based assessments by paying very close attention to one major factor: reaction time to feedback (Popham, 2009). Reaction time is the time it takes a student to internalize and act on assessment feedback. By shortening the reaction time, teachers can create a more process-based assessment culture in their classrooms (Wiliam, 2011).

Shortening Reaction Time

While important in all grade levels and across all subject areas, reaction time is a relative concept. In language arts classrooms, short reaction time may be a week, while in mathematics it may be seconds. To discover the appropriate reaction time, teachers must scrutinize the time between instruction and assessment completion that produces the most active student response to feedback. If this timing is spaced correctly, students will retain knowledge and skill longer than if presented with feedback at a disproportionate time to the assessment (Wiliam, 2011).

By simply creating proficiency-based gradations of learning and lowering the reaction time to feedback, a teacher is 90 percent of the way to making assessment process based. The other 10 percent happens naturally during the maturation of the team's conversation. See the following sample team time line, and watch how the assessment becomes a process.

- **September 15:** Team creates proficiency-based targets. Team creates measurable and proficient targets that represent four levels of proficiency.

- **October 1:** Team creates assessments from the levels of proficiency-based targets. Team uses the levels of the gradation and uses the language of the target to create the assessments and lessons.

- **October 25:** Team shortens the assessments. If created correctly, assessments naturally become shorter and more formative due to the alignment to the target. This shortening happens because the assessment is now producing the best evidence possible to assess students. Longer assessments are not useful anymore.

- **November 5:** Team creates more reflective lessons. Since assessments are now shorter and smaller in scope, the lesson has time to include more reflection opportunities. These opportunities ask students to use feedback in a timely manner, thus increasing their value in the classroom. Reflecting and using feedback are so integrated with the assessment process now that they appear as indistinguishable events to the learner.

- **December 17:** Team decides that reflection is of more value than ever before. Since there is now no delineation between reflecting and assessing, assessment is the process of reflection and nothing more.

Consider the following scenarios and how a teacher may shorten the reaction time to feedback for students.

- **Scenario 1:** Mr. Smith has his students read the feedback comments on each assessment. The feedback identifies content deficits and learning targets that need work. Mr. Smith provides a website for students to go to for help if needed before the next test.

This example, while common practice in many classrooms, actually has a long reaction time to feedback as Mr. Smith leaves an undefined time line for students to react to the feedback to the assessment. Mr. Smith provides support but does not ask students to do anything with the feedback in a timely manner. Therefore, this model has a long reaction time line, which minimizes the impact for learning.

- **Scenario 2:** Mr. Rodriguez has students use a postassessment checklist. The students mark which questions they got right and explain why. The students also mark which questions they got wrong and explain why. Furthermore, the students write down what targets they still need to work on. Students then use this guide to go to a website to remediate the targets by the next week.

In this example, common reflective practice in most classrooms has a short reaction time to feedback but fails to have students act on the feedback. A student simply checking off "I got it wrong" and telling why does not provide the correct foundation from which the student can act. Mr. Rodriguez again provides support and even provides an opportunity for students to react to the feedback, but the reaction is too simplistic, and the time line on which to act again is too long. Therefore, while this model had reaction, the reaction was outcomes based (right or wrong) with a long reaction time line, which minimizes the impact for learning.

- **Scenario 3:** Ms. Lee has students record their thoughts *during* the assessment itself. The students are required to record not only the answer but also their thinking that goes into each problem. After the assessment time is up, Ms. Lee has students compare their thinking with that of other students. After reviewing with the class some patterns of thinking that are wrong and some that are correct, Ms. Lee asks the students to perform the assessment again. Students then work together in small groups to create one final assessment that Ms. Lee will use as evidence of learning.

In this final example, Ms. Lee takes a new approach. She uses the assessment as a process, asking students to self-assess during the exam and then teaching the students to self-reflect and sift through the patterns of thought they used to attack the problems on the assessment. Once she has focused the class on her expected methods of solving the problem, she then asks the students to immediately reperform the assessment with the feedback they received. This example shows a short reaction time to feedback and ultimately has a high impact on their performance because Ms. Lee has the students use the feedback to perform an assessment.

Assessment will naturally become more of a process as the proficiency-based target seeps deeper into instruction. The more teachers use proficiency-based targets in instruction, the more they will assess students formatively. This ultimately gives teachers the realization that assessment in process form can be more valuable than assessment in product form.

Combination 3: Assessment Structure and Frequency

One of the more exciting moments during the incubation phase is when teachers and collaborative teams begin to think differently about the intersection between their assessment frequency and the internal structure of their assessments. As they do so, we find that traditional viewpoints on scaffolding begin to fall apart.

We believe firmly that the way assessment is traditionally implemented is counterproductive to creating a culture of proficiency-based assessment. Consider the visual representation of current instructional and assessment practices in figure 3.4. Each white dot represents an event that must be successfully completed to get to the next white dot.

Figure 3.4: Current time line of instruction and assessment.

The prevailing belief is that if we can move students through a linear pathway to mastery of a particular target, we increase the likelihood that students will get to the next level of understanding. Once students have mastered a particular learning element or skill, they can move to the next level—*after* demonstrating success of the previous learning element. This linear assessment model would be easily recognizable to many students: two formative assessments, a quiz, a project, a summative exam, a retake, and instruction nestled in between.

While we cannot expect teachers during the incubation phase to completely abandon their assessment practices, we believe that we can move closer to a proficiency-based model by considering the following two questions (Wiggins & McTighe, 2005).

1. Do we have *enough* evidence of student performance?

2. Do we have the *right* evidence of student performance?

These two questions force the creation of a proper assessment structure, which is based on two components (Marzano, 2010): (1) the time line component, as mentioned previously, which helps answer "How much evidence is enough?" and (2) the structural component of the assessment, which refers to the sections or segments of the assessment. This structural component helps answer the question, "Do we have enough of the *right* evidence?" (Wiggins & McTighe, 2005).

In the diagram in figure 3.5, the shaded horizontal line represents the question, "Do we have enough evidence?" with each circle representing an assessment event: formative assessments (FA), quizzes, projects, summative exams, and retakes. Teachers must plan assessments in this fashion to ensure that they have *enough* evidence to accurately determine how well a student is performing.

The second component, shown in white in figure 3.5, represents the internal structure of assessment. This white line shows how an assessment must replicate the gradations of the proficiency-based learning target we talked about earlier.

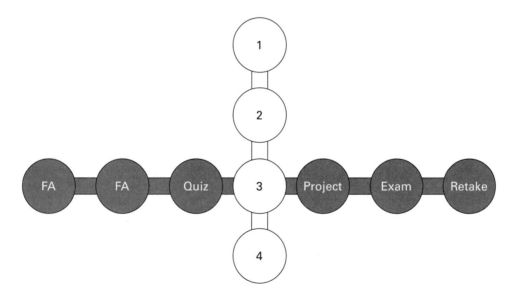

Figure 3.5: The merging of the two assessment time lines.

Let's see how this concept plays out in a mathematics class. Figure 3.6 (page 92) features an algebra quiz that was *not* developed with these two components in mind.

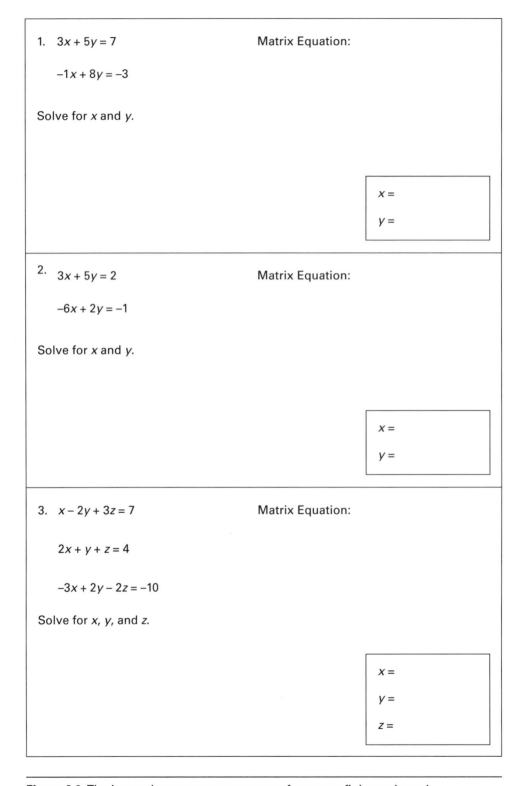

1. $3x + 5y = 7$ Matrix Equation:

    $-1x + 8y = -3$

    Solve for x and y.

                                                    $x =$
                                                    $y =$

2. $3x + 5y = 2$ Matrix Equation:

    $-6x + 2y = -1$

    Solve for x and y.

                                                    $x =$
                                                    $y =$

3. $x - 2y + 3z = 7$ Matrix Equation:

    $2x + y + z = 4$

    $-3x + 2y - 2z = -10$

    Solve for x, y, and z.

                                                    $x =$
                                                    $y =$
                                                    $z =$

Figure 3.6: The internal structure component of a nonproficiency-based mathematics assessment.

The gradations for this exam are as follows.

4—Use various types of matrices to solve any advanced system of equations correctly.

3—Use various types of matrices to solve any system of equations correctly.

2—Use various types of matrices to solve some systems of equations correctly.

1—Use various types of matrices to solve specific systems of equations correctly with help.

The first concern is that the target is not proficiency based and, secondly, is missing measurable language. Without these things, it will be extremely difficult for an assessment to function effectively on both of the assessment time lines.

Another concern with this example is that this assessment contains only one level of the gradation, level 3. Assessments, to assess proficiency accurately, must capture *all* levels of the learning gradation (Marzano, 2010). Therefore, any assessment that is employed should allow for a student to produce evidence at all levels of the proficiency-based target. That means a section for level 4, a section for level 3, and a section for levels 2 and 1. Without creating assessments with these two planes in mind, teachers will never have *enough* of the *right* evidence to assess students accurately.

Now, let's look at this same assessment, but let's see how the same team used the two proficiency-based assessment components to create a more effective assessment. The first step is to use a proficiency-based target like the following.

4—Given a set of related data, generate a matrix representation including all key features.

3—Given a system of equations, generate a matrix representation including all key features.

2—Given a system of equations, generate a matrix representation including specific key features.

1—Given a system of equations and key features, generate a matrix representation.

With measurability and proficiency existing in the target, now teachers have the foundation to create effective assessments. Effective assessments capture all levels of the gradation, not just one (Marzano, 2010). We see the updated assessment in figure 3.7 (pages 94–95).

1. $3x + 5y = 7$

   $-1x + 8y = -3$

   Solve for x and y.

   Matrix Equation:

   $x =$

   $y =$

2. $3x + 5y = 2$

   $-6x + 2y = -1$

   Solve for x and y.

   Matrix Equation:

   $x =$

   $y =$

3. $x - 2y + 3z = 7$

   $2x + y + z = 4$

   $-3x + 2y - 2z = -10$

   Solve for x, y, and z.

   Matrix Equation:

   $x =$

   $y =$

   $z =$

At the start of the school year, the sixth-, seventh-, and eighth-grade classes purchased supplies. The sixth-grade class spent a total of $93.25, the seventh-grade class spent a total of $79.50, and the eighth-grade class spent a total of $64. The number of each item purchased is listed in the following table. Determine how much each item costs.

	Boxes of Markers	Boxes of Pencils	Boxes of Binders
Sixth Grade	3	4	5
Seventh Grade	5	1	4
Eighth Grade	7	3	2

System of Equations:

Matrix Equation:

	Cost per box
Markers	
Pencils	
Binders	

Figure 3.7: The internal structure component of a proficiency-based mathematics assessment.

When assessments function effectively, not only in the structure but in timing and pacing, teachers will gather more of the right evidence of student learning and have more flexibility in applying the assessment during instruction. To determine the correct timing and pacing of proficiency-based assessment, teams use a timing chart to better diagnose how much evidence is enough and when enough is enough. See figure 3.8 for a sample chart.

	Week 1	Week 2	Week 3
Proficiency-Based Target 1	Proficiency-based assessment event		Proficiency-based assessment event
Proficiency-Based Target 2		Proficiency-based assessment event	
Proficiency-Based Target 3	Proficiency-based assessment event	Proficiency-based assessment event	
Proficiency-Based Target 4			Proficiency-based assessment event

Figure 3.8: Sample timing chart.

To create this timing chart, teams list the proficiency-based targets on the far-left column. Then, the teams determine how to divide time increments for assessing their targets (in this case it is by week) and place those along the top of the chart. Then, the proficiency-based assessment events that will occur are recorded to capture evidence on the targets. This chart is extremely useful when teams are asking if they have enough evidence for a proficiency-based target. When a teacher or team can answer this question confidently, then proficiency-based assessment can function properly.

Combination 4: Instruction and Assessment

In combination 2, we discussed the instruction and the process of *student* reflection; here, we focus on instruction and the *teacher's* approach to assessment. If we use proficiency-based targets, then assessment and instruction essentially become the same thing (Wiliam, 2011). When instruction and assessment become one and the same, there is simply no need to verify student learning with a product-based assessment, because a teacher is constantly interpreting student-produced evidence against the proficiency-based target. They are the same thing because when a teacher instructs with a proficiency-based target, both entities now serve the same academic purpose, which is *reacting to student evidence*. This idea is in contrast to the linear nature of instruction and assessment we see in traditional education.

Understanding the Problem With the Linear Lesson

Our current linear model of instruction exists because it is organizationally effective and attempts to ensure that all students learn, not because it is the most effective way to teach. The main advantage is that it takes a naturally chaotic process (student learning) and imposes order; however, it does so at the expense of the student's learning. We traditionally see this type of linear lesson model like figure 3.9.

Step 1: Present target to students.

Step 2: Present content to students.

Step 3: Engage students with target through simple tasks.

Step 4: Engage students with target through moderate tasks.

Step 5: Engage students with target through complex tasks.

Step 6: Review to verify learning.

Step 7: Assess to verify learning.

Step 8: React to student evidence (react to assessment data).

Figure 3.9: Traditional lesson sequence.

In this linear lesson model, instruction and assessment act separately; instruction acts as delivery, and assessment acts as verification. The major drawback to the scaffolding model in figure 3.9 is its focus on outcomes and success indicators. Students must be completely successful in step 3 before they move on to step 4 and the same from step 4 to step 5. This means that since students are always successful, there is less need for reflection, and the importance of assessing during instruction is downplayed, and the teacher then simply employs assessment in step 7 to verify that learning happened.

When successful outcomes are the focus, as in this model, learning becomes a desert, devoid of mistakes, errors, misconceptions, perceptions, and experience—all the good stuff that lifelong learning is reliant on. If teachers always structure lessons in this manner, students will simply try to *match* what the model outcome is. Or, in other words, they will try to match what will satisfy the task rather than what will satisfy their thinking (Schoemaker, 2011).

By creating linear learning environments, we actually remove any potential for students reaching their learning threshold, an area of high cognitive dissonance with high potential for learning to occur (Schoemaker, 2011). Since the lesson is segmented into highly achievable portions, students never reach their personal potential for learning simply because they are always successful.

Merging Instruction and Assessment

Proficiency-based assessment dictates an alternative to the linear lesson. A proficiency-based lesson is a lesson framework based on unsized and undefined configurations that are centered on proficiency. This means that we must dynamically use evidence produced from the students during the lesson to produce appropriate instruction and assessment opportunities. This idea challenges even some of the best teachers when asked to describe what this might look like. Danielson (2011) describes it best when she describes using assessment in instruction: "Even after careful planning, however, the teacher must weave monitoring of student learning seamlessly into the lesson, using a variety of techniques" (p. 62). This means that as teachers we must resist the urge to react to student needs through predetermined strategies and action but instead flexibly react to student production, using all purposeful strategies that we possess. Think about it this way: coaches don't simply rely on the prede-termined game plan they developed before a game—they react to the situations that the game itself presents using a variety of strategies they have at their disposal. Teaching is no different in this regard, and we advocate that teachers take this same approach to formatively assessing and instructing students. First, make a game plan (proficiency-based learning target), and then simply react to the students are giving you (proficiency-based instruction). When teachers use this approach, we get a far different model of teaching than our earlier linear lesson, as shown in figure 3.10.

Step 1: Present target to students.

Step 2: Students interact with target through reflective activities.

Step 3: React to evidence while students are engaging with all
levels of gradation using content and skill.

Figure 3.10: Proficiency-based lesson sequence.

In a proficiency-based lesson, a proficiency-based target is used to assess students as well as guide instruction. This not only eliminates unnecessary steps in the teaching process, but it also allows for more flexible instruction, which mirrors how students learn. When the proficiency-based target acts as assessment, instruction, and curriculum, the lessons become student centered, and the learner is more involved in all three of these elements.

To create lessons based on proficiency instead of outcomes, we must follow these guidelines.

- **Instruction has no shape or size:** Realize that lessons are not small systematic increments to success, but rather undefined reflective actions or events designed to direct students toward proficiency. As we know from the previous chapter, predetermined size and shape of a lesson have the potential to promote an outcomes-based environment that can actually slow down learning. The teacher must *mold* the lesson while it is happening (Danielson, 2007), sculpting the direction of learning based on student-produced evidence at that moment, using the gradations of the target as a map guiding the lesson. By fashioning the lesson based on the student production instead of predetermined events or time lines, the learning environment changes dramatically. It becomes so flexible, so malleable, and so dynamic that authentic learning experiences are the norm.

- **Instruction is not delivery, it is reaction:** Teachers should assess or, as we say in proficiency-based assessment, *react to student evidence during the* *lesson* using an undetermined variety of formative assessments (Marzano, 2010). Teachers must possess a flexible literacy of assessment type (Badders, 2000), assessment purpose, and assessment logistics to have any hope of selecting the most appropriate type of learning events for their students (Ainsworth & Viegut, 2006).

- **Instruction occurs inside the target:** What proficiency-based assessment is essentially asking teachers to do is to "crawl inside" their target to teach. What we mean is that a teacher must use his or her gradation of learning *during* teaching (Moss & Brookhart, 2012). Once teachers are using the gradation, or they are "inside the target," they can immediately interpret and simultaneously react to student–produced evidence to move the lesson forward. A visual representation of this concept is found in table 3.2.

Table 3.2: Merging of Proficiency-Based Targets and Proficiency-Based Instruction

Level of Proficiency	Description and Measurement
4	*Exceeds expectations:* Students in this category consistently and substantially exceed requirements and perform at maximum levels of effectiveness.
	Instruction (Reaction to Student Evidence)
3	*Meets expectations:* Students in this category consistently meet requirements of the target and perform in a fully expected and reliable manner.
	Instruction (Reaction to Student Evidence)
2	*Approaching expectations:* Students in this category may demonstrate emerging levels of proficient comprehension or skill development.
	Instruction (Reaction to Student Evidence)
1	*Emerging understanding:* Students in this category may demonstrate basic levels of comprehension or skill development.

We know this is a sample gradation that has generic language; however, we want to bring your attention to each aspect of the diagram. The numbers on the left represent the four gradations of the proficiency-based target. The descriptions in black next to the numbers outline the expected level of proficiency and how the teacher is measuring said proficiency. Lastly, the bold rows contain the instruction and assessment of (or the teacher's reaction to) student evidence. By using the gradation in instruction, a teacher can now react uniquely to each student's needs by employing the instruction and assessment (in the bold text sections of table 3.2) that are appropriate to move each student between levels of the target.

For example, if a student is producing evidence that fits the level 3 proficiency levels, the teacher already has verified (assessed) the level of learning, because she or he knows the student is at level 3, based on what the student is saying about or doing with the content. Since the teacher knows this, she or he can now employ the instructional reactions that reside between levels 3 and 4 in order to propel the student to level 4. The teacher can use this practice to quickly and effectively determine where a student or class is and propel the instruction in the appropriate direction.

Some educators to whom we have presented this idea feel uncomfortable that the verification step is missing from this diagram. However, it is not actually missing; it is simply happening *as* instruction. By instructionally manipulating proficiency-based gradations, teachers can verify student learning simultaneously as they decide which instructional strategy to employ. Merging instruction and assessment is a theme that will continue in the next stages of learning and is a central idea of proficiency-based learning.

Key Points

Following are key points from the chapter that readers should review to ensure they have a firm grasp on the content.

- The team members should see that effective targets are interconnected with the development of instructional improvements and brainstorm instructional ideas that apply this interdependent relationship.

- The team members can make use of the three-target test to ensure that each target describes one type of thinking or skill.

- During incubation, teachers consider how assessment will best allow a student to demonstrate target proficiency.

Chapter 4

Insight

The insight phase is one of the most exciting stages during the creative process. This is the point where the lightbulb goes on and the mind exclaims, "Aha!" and the adrenaline kicks in. There is a strong recognition of understanding, or a connection is made; there is a point of realization, invention, or innovation. A foothold toward change is identified, motivating individuals and teams to move forward in their work.

When we are working in collaboration, we want to recognize that these insights and realizations occur at different points for different teammates. However, the important point to remember is that through the preparation and incubation phases, insights and aha! moments have been developing. Collaborative discussions, questioning, and even pushback have been fueling the development of associations and that ultimate aha! An individual might beat someone to the punch, but the collaborative interaction of the group is vital to that verbalized insight. If we want to see real change, we need the input of all team members to reach the aha! moment.

Working collaboratively is essential to moving the needle toward changes in assessment. At this point in the creative process stage, aha! takes a moment to sink in. It is tempting to move immediately to the evaluation phase and ask, "Is that really a good idea or not?" and to immediately believe your team is onto something huge that is going to change what we know about education. Sorry to burst the bubble, but that is often not the case. Edison's team on the lightbulb went through hundreds of failed insights. So, let's slow down a bit with our team and analyze how the insight is emerging, and how we can go about supporting our team at this exciting juncture.

Following are three key points to remember during the insight phase.

1. During the incubation phase, the team members generated ideas. During the insight phase, they identify the idea that makes the most sense to them based on their expertise—the idea they are most invested in implementing. It is important to practice risk taking during this stage—teams cannot fear making mistakes as long as they have enough time to reflect on revisions. Teams need to feel support to make a decision in order to move forward.

2. An insight might be good or bad—no one knows quite yet. The insight will be evaluated during the next phase; however, as teams collaborate, expertise and smart considerations interact to identify which insight the team will act on.

3. At this point, creativity is highly recursive. Team members may be revisiting other phases simultaneously. That's a good sign.

As you read our team's story, pay attention to how insights related to proficiency-based assessment emerge in the following ways.

*   The members of the team draw a clear relationship among their instructional responses to the following four questions: (1) What are the expectations for students related to a given topic or a given skill? (2) How will they know whether they've met expectations? (3) What thinking were they relying on if they did not learn the topic or skill? and (4) How will they extend that learning if they already have competency?

*   The team members are identifying clear relationships among curriculum, instruction, and assessment because their discussions are more sophisticated around the four Is: *intangible*, *instantaneous*, *inseparable*, and *individualized*.

*   The leadership supports the team members' recognition of an insight, provides a supportive critique, and begins to help them take steps toward implementation.

Our Team's Story

During the time between team meetings, Bruce and his colleagues constantly shared realizations about the work they were implementing around proficiency-based assessment. They exchanged thoughts and setbacks informally. The work around scaling healthy targets challenged each team member's instructional practices and everyone's mindset. As they shared with the group, Bruce listened closely and paid attention to make sure there was clarity among team members and that their shared understanding and collaborative team decisions were being implemented. He worked to be supportive and encouraging in these conversations, and he recognized and valued everyone's level of communication and trust.

At the next full team meeting, Bruce opened with an informal check-in about the changes they were all trying to make. He asked the team to share their insights regarding the work of the new learning target and answer this question: "How did the implementation of the new learning targets lead to new embedded formative assessment practices in the classroom, such as retakes, shorter assessments, or our use of common formative assessments?"

Morrison and Vaughn started with comments about how it was difficult to manage all the paperwork now that students could self-reflect and retake assessments to demonstrate growth toward proficiency and mastery; likewise, they mentioned how much more their team members were reviewing the common formative data together.

Joni agreed, "It's difficult to build the personal capacity to check all the students' formative work and grade an assessment."

Britney jumped in as well, "I feel that there is some good stuff here that is making me think, but it seems to get a bit repetitive. For the reflection piece, I have students check which targets they don't know at the end of each lesson, and then they go to my website to remediate. That has been very helpful, but it is the same process each time. Is that OK?"

Joni said, "I am struggling with what to do with my students when some know it and some don't. I simply can't help all groups in my class at the same time."

With this instant momentum, Bruce decided to dive right in. He said, "I think we need to revisit how our views of proficiency-based targets are related to assessment and student learning. There were some questions we used before, but I can't seem to remember them."

Morrison inquired, "You mean these?" He pulled out a sheet he received years ago on a professional learning day that included the following questions based on the work of DuFour, DuFour, Eaker, and Karhanek (2010).

- What do we want students to know?
- How will we know that they know it?
- What will we do if they don't learn it?
- What will we do if they do know it?

Bruce said, "I think these questions are important, but I think they are misinterpreted by many teachers as a narrowed view of assessment."

Joni wondered, "What do you mean?"

Vaughn noted, "These questions were at the root of much of my work in graduate school. In what ways do you think they are misinterpreted?"

Bruce answered, "When I met with other team leaders who are working with proficiency-based assessment, many of their teams struggled with these questions. They asked their teams to answer each of those four listed questions, and this is what they generally said." Bruce displayed the questions and the responses.

- What do we want students to know? Topics and themes

- How will we know that they know it? Summative and formative assessments

- What will we do if they don't learn it? Remediation, more practice, review sessions

- What will we do if they do know it? Move on to new topic

Joni wondered, "I'm curious. I might have answered the same way, but now I'm thinking that we should be considering these questions to have a deeper purpose that teams keep missing."

"I agree," said Bruce. "What we should be asking is this: What questions do we need to ask? How will they know if they have met the expectation? What thinking were they relying on if they didn't learn it? How will they extend that learning if they have competency already? If teachers ask these questions it will lead students to begin asking themselves these questions: Do I know what the desired stated expectation is? Am I where I am supposed to be? If not, what thinking led me astray? If yes, am I fluent or flexible in my application of skill or knowledge?"

Bruce continued, "By beginning with questions, proficiency is driven to the center of the instructional exchanges between teacher and student. Also these questions have a dual purpose. First, they require that students know what proficiency is, but they also require that students reflect with a directed purpose. By shaping the four critical questions in this way, proficiency is placed at the core of instruction and generates an importance for student reflection in the classroom."

Morrison said, "While these questions are important, I think the instruction piece is still really significant to consider right now."

Bruce answered, "I agree, but these questions help guide how we instruct. They help uncover three important elements of instruction. The three principles of proficiency-based assessment are (1) desired expectation, (2) current state, and (3) gap thinking. If these three principles exist in every lesson, then the students will get in the habit of asking themselves the right questions to improve learning."

"I'm not quite following you, Bruce. What does that mean?" asked Morrison.

Bruce told the team that even though the concepts of desired state, current state, and gap thinking are not new, there are still three major flaws in assessment that can get in the way of these focused principles.

Bruce began to summarize: "One flaw is that teachers don't know their desired state. They have little awareness of the expectation of competency for a topic, content, or skill. In short, teachers create nonproficiency-based targets. Poor targets force proficiency out of view of educators, and they create unreliable assessments, make for stagnate lesson plans, and lengthen rigorous curricula. However, they can avoid these concerns by reaching clarity on their own expectations of students. As we discussed in our earlier meetings, our targets were not stating our expectations; they were simply communicating themes. Therefore, we were unable to see them as instructional mechanisms."

"The second error is that most teachers don't teach with the students' current state of thinking. The majority of research will tell us the importance of capturing student reflection, but most teachers don't allow students' self-reflection to guide individual learning. This is a concern that proficiency-based assessment addresses. We teach our students to find clarity around their current state of learning. We need to value a student's current state of thinking as it pertains to a particular target.

"Finally, the third area we need to pay attention to is the significant and smart work being done around the response to intervention (RTI) model. The gap between students' understanding and what the teacher is teaching them is consistently viewed as a concern. When there is a lack of proficiency, interventions are needed in order to help bridge the gap. This commitment is an important one to consider as we think about the relationship proficiency-based assessment should have in relation to RTI."

Britney replied, "I agree. A strong intervention can allow us to uncover the reason for the gap in thinking. The two should really work together to help support every student."

Bruce provided an example and said, "If a student is deficient in, say, adequately citing key details in familiar narrative passages, traditional teaching will say, 'Identify the deficiency and remediate with the resources of time, extra practice, and repetition.'"

Bruce continued, "Proficiency-based assessment asks us to find the deficiency in the gap and capture student thinking that led to the gap. This is done by creating reflective lessons that constantly use the students' current state of thinking and asking them how they would develop a desired state. It's important to resist asking them what is different between their state and the desired state, as this focuses on deficiency. If we ask students what is different between the two states, continuing with the example of adequately citing key details in a familiar narrative passage, students will state discrete components that need to be reviewed. For example, 'I didn't know that word, so I need to review the steps to finding key details.'

"However, if we ask students how they might turn their current state into the desired state, a teacher will expose what learned ideas or conceptions a student is attempting to combine in order to achieve the desired state. It is this thinking we want to expose. Using our example again in this way, we would expect responses like 'I would look for the author's tone and use that to discover key details,' which is a great line of thinking and may be correct. But it may also expose bad lines of thinking such as 'I would look for words that seem thematically connected to one another and say that those are the key details'—not necessarily the thinking that is going to produce the learning we need." Bruce finished, "These new types of instructional exchanges will expose trains of thought that are healthy and should be followed or that need to be stopped and redirected before these roots take hold and cause the student to rely on faulty lines of logic and thought."

"In other words," said Morrison, "this work will help us to better understand where and when students get stuck in their train of thought."

Joni wondered, "OK, but how do we do this in our instruction?"

Bruce said, "I asked the same question to other proficiency-based colleagues. Past instructional trainings and publications focused on a model of learning where students sit and absorb content. We want to find the deficiencies between the desired state of the target skill and the current state. For this reason, I think what we need to do is take more of a reflective approach to teaching and hear more from each student."

Vaughn asked, "More reflective?"

Britney said, "I think students should be able to identify what they know and don't know, not just us. They should be able to reflect on that on their own, shouldn't they?"

Morrison spoke, "So how do we do that? With these desired states and current states, what does the target have to do with all this?"

Britney interjected, "Wait, I think I am starting to get this. The learning target is the teacher's expectation, the desired state. So that is why we rewrote our targets with measurability and proficiency. And the current state is what a student thinks about his or her aptitude and growth. We as teachers can capture this state any way we decide, but we must teach with it, not simply verify it. Then, lastly, we must create lessons that are structured reflectively for students to review how they would turn their current state into a desired state."

Joni exclaimed, "Yes! I had the same realization!"

Vaughn said, smiling but a bit nervous, "OK, I am beginning to see it now, but this is still a lot to process."

Bruce said, "I think about the first step this way: if our classes are 80 percent instruction, and 20 percent reflection, simply reverse it. Make it 80 percent reflection and 20 percent instruction. This mindset will get you going. It's called the reverse 80–20 principle."

After a long pause, Morrison sighed. "Wow—that is a big shift."

Vaughn came back, "Maybe you all can visualize how to do this, but this is my first year, and I just can't understand how to do this. I will need your help."

Joni asked, "So how does this all affect assessment, curriculum, and instruction?"

Bruce paused a moment, then gave the team another big nugget to chew on. "Well, in proficiency-based assessment, the claim is that they are all the same thing."

Britney spoke first, "OK, I see how curriculum and instruction are close relatives, but assessment still seems like a separate thing to me."

Morrison shared his thoughts carefully. "Well," he said, "let's see if I got this. If we have healthy targets, they are curriculum. They tell us everything we need to know about what we are teaching. Assessment basically becomes the ongoing interaction with a desired state—well, target, and the current state of the students—and instruction becomes the reflective structure in which this interaction occurs."

Joni smiled and said, "That is great! Wow! I think I'm finally starting to see how we're getting somewhere."

Bruce finished, "If we follow these insights from this meeting, we will get very close to the ultimate merging of curriculum, instruction, and assessment. This would really help us to fully implement proficiency-based assessment."

As the team started to pack up, Morrison asked, "So where to next? If we have these resources and realizations ready, what do we do now?"

Joni spoke up, "I think we should plan a lesson, prototype it, reflect on it, and talk about it at our next staff development meeting—maybe even present our findings. That way we can evaluate our efforts and compare each other's thinking."

The team agreed that this would be the best approach. They decided on their next action step: to plan an effective lesson that demonstrated their new thinking, implement it, and reflect on it.

The Four Insights of Proficiency-Based Assessment

In this phase of learning, a team begins to develop exciting insights into their practices. While the team in our story is focusing its efforts on proficiency-based assessment, the members uncover four very important insights into their curricular, instructional, and assessment practices.

1. How students think is more important than what they don't know.

2. Assessment does not verify learning; it supports it.

3. There are three essential elements of teaching.

4. The three essential questions of assessment for learning have deeper corollary questions.

Insight 1: How Students Think Is More Important Than What They Don't Know

In outcomes-based classrooms, teachers present material, students may or may not get feedback on homework or quizzes, and after a summative testing experience, students are assigned a grade that supposedly represents their acquired knowledge level (Guskey & Jung, 2013; Wiggins & McTighe, 2005; Wiliam, 2011). We believe that one of the major reasons why this pattern still exists in many districts, schools, and classrooms is that we tend to focus on students' *de*ficiencies rather than their emerging *pro*ficiencies. In deficiency-focused classrooms, students become overly reliant on their teachers to help fill in the learning gaps they develop. Through this insight teachers can help students begin to rely on themselves to learn. So how do we help students focus on emerging thinking rather than identified discrepancies?

Student Reflection

In proficiency-based classrooms, lessons are organized around student self-observations and continuous reflection guided by proficiency-based targets (Chappuis, 2009). Teachers are teaching students how to reflect, how to react to those reflections, and how to act on those reflections for learning growth (Chappuis, 2009). Through the integration of a proficiency-based assessment we learn that assessment is the interplay in students' self-observation and a stated competency expectation (Stiggins et al., 2004).

In proficiency-based assessment classrooms, reflection is at the heart of the lesson design. All instructional activities revolve around opportunities for students to reflect on their level of understanding or skill development in relation to a proficiency-based target (Stiggins & Chappuis, 2012). Every day, in every classroom, multiple times within a class period, students give and receive feedback on their thinking and reflection on the learning targets (Moss & Brookhart, 2012). This allows students to discover the quality of their thinking (and learning) by observing their own performance on a gradation of learning.

By using proficiency-based targets and offering reflective questions that ensure a learning relationship with the proficiency aspects of the target, a teacher can help students create a reflective relationship with targets. There are three key questions that can ensure this relationship (Martin-Kniep, 2000; Moss & Brookhart, 2012).

1. **Does the target clearly outline what is expected of me?** Students must know if their thinking about the topic is profound or simple. When students have clarity on what is expected of them, they can accurately gauge the depth and impact of every thought they have. When students are asked to be self-assessors, they cannot accurately do so without this clarity of expected quality (Stiggins et al., 2004). When proficiency is clear, learners can accurately assess the impact of their thinking.

    In our world history target example, *Using examples from class I can effectively explain the main political, economic, and social causes of World War I in a written analysis*, students who have clarity can now ask themselves questions like "Is my analysis convincing?" and "Are the details I am associating with this topic the best details I can use?"

    When students review their own work in relation to a target in this way, the learning that takes place is more potent and lasting. Students can only do this policing if they have clarity of the expected proficiency.

2. **How does my thinking connect to the target?** Let's look at our target example, *Using examples from class I can effectively explain the main political, economic, and social causes of World War I in a written analysis*. Generally speaking, what happens in many classrooms is students tend to focus their attention on the *explain* element of the target. Since proficiency-based assessment supports students in discovering the proficiency aspects of the target instead of the verb, students can now begin to gain perspective on the quality of their own learning. In our

example, proficiency-based teachers have their students connect thinking to the words *effectively* and *main*. When this happens, the student creates an accurate learning relationship with the target, and student learning now has a heightened focus on proficiency. For example, students who focus their learning on the word *effectively* may ask themselves: "Am I effectively explaining what I want to?" or "Can I see effectiveness in my work?" or "Have I effectively explained all of the main ideas?"

3. **Can I use the target to reflect on and assess my work?** Is the relationship between my thinking and the target clear and crisp? Are there any unnecessary details that I have relied on to create meaning? Having students search for a clear logic pattern in the relationship between their thinking and the proficiency language of the target allows them to determine whether their work is proficient. Students must use the target to reflect on the thinking they are using in a coherent way to accurately process the material. In other words, using the target to aid in reflection actually helps lessen the "white noise" of learning.

In the world history example, *Using examples from class I can effectively explain the main political, economic, and social causes of World War I in a written analysis*, if students have created a learning relationship with the targeted words *effectively* and *main*, then they can take reflective stances similar to "Do the main causes I have learned and the related details clearly satisfy the target?" Normally, this is a question teachers ask when they are verifying learning, but now when a target is used for reflection, it allows students to ask these types of questions themselves!

Student Recognition of Learning Thresholds

As lifelong Chicago Bulls fans, we loved watching Michael Jordan and company win six NBA titles during the 1990s. Funny enough, we loved watching their commercials too! In one of our favorites, Jordan is walking through the tunnel of the United Center, and he remarks:

> I've missed more than nine thousand shots in my career. I've lost almost three hundred games. Twenty-six times, I've been trusted to take the game-winning shot and missed. I've failed over and over and over again in my life. And that is why I succeed. (as cited in JayMJ23, n.d.)

We find it fascinating that while some of us fear failure, others find tremendous benefits in the experience of repeated failure.

Paul Schoemaker (2011), an expert in decision science and behavioral economics, reminds us of the importance of failure in his wonderful book *Brilliant Mistakes*. In it, he suggests:

> One needs to be judicious about the trade-offs between the cost of making an error and the potential benefits of learning. This is especially difficult if you don't know the limitations of your knowledge base (how far you are off the mark). (p. 515)

Making mistakes, failing, and learning from that experience help students to find their *learning threshold*—a cognitive area just beyond a student's current state of learning with a high potential for learning and growth (Schoemaker, 2011). This is the area some may call an area of dissonance, but we call it the optimal zone for optimal learning. In proficiency-based assessment, students must constantly remain in this area to see how close they are to the proficiency-based target.

While learning thresholds are rather difficult for teachers and students to discover, a proficiency-based target can help a teacher push students to the appropriate learning threshold by simply following the gradation of proficiency. By keeping feedback related to the gradation level a student is *trying to reach*, a teacher can help students stay in this optimal zone for learning, at their learning threshold.

To see how a teacher ushers students toward their learning thresholds, we can look at our world history target example, *Using examples from class I can effectively explain the main political, economic, and social causes of World War I in a written analysis*. A teacher would help students find their learning thresholds by saying things like "I see what you are writing there, and it is on the right track, but can you see how that last cause you listed is not a main cause?" or "I see you have all the main causes, but remember, for it to be an effective explanation, your answer should include [particular content aspect]."

Having students interact with all levels of the proficiency-based target at the same time reveals learning thresholds. Teachers cannot simply teach in a systematic linear fashion but must alternate the lesson between different gradations to drive students toward their learning boundary. Teachers must *intentionally* swing the lesson between gradations of the proficiency target of learning. While each gradation can contain an infinite amount of proficiency language, the following proficiency language combinations have proven to be effective in the discovery of learning thresholds.

- **Structured tasks and unstructured tasks:** An example in a mathematics course would be alternating the lesson between labeling graphs with preloaded data sets (structured task) and drawing graphs from data sets (unstructured task).

- **Definite contexts and indefinite contexts:** An example in a world language course would be an oral assignment that alternates between speaking about what one did yesterday at school (definite context) and what one did yesterday in general (indefinite context).

- **Proficient content and rigorous content:** An example in a language arts course would be alternating a reading lesson between reading a *Hamlet* vocabulary with direct translation and meaning (proficient content) and reading a *Hamlet* vocabulary with idiomatic and implied meaning (rigorous content).

- **Familiar situations and unfamiliar situations:** An example in a science course would be alternating a physics lab lesson between how gravity works on Earth (familiar situation) and how gravity works on other planets (unfamiliar situation).

- **Low-stakes performance and high-stakes performance:** An example in a language arts course would be alternating a writing lesson between writing a thesis (low stakes) and writing a free-response question (high stakes).

Let's be clear about one thing: by alternating the lesson, we do not mean moving in baby steps from the definite to the indefinite or scaffolding from familiar to unfamiliar situations. We mean that students must interact completely and directly with multiple levels of the gradation to produce evidence that represents the true current state of learning. By doing this, a teacher can shake the lesson enough to spill out evidence of learning thresholds. Shaking learning means that the teacher constantly changes the instruction according to the gradations of the proficiency-based target to force a reflective experience for the student, which then produces evidence of learning. But remember, finding a learning threshold is not about keeping students in dissonance. When teachers identify students' learning thresholds, they have actually assessed them (Wiliam, 2011) and subsequently must attempt to solidify proficiency in the emerging gradation of the target. Once all parties have identified a learning threshold, assessment has occurred. Identifying a learning threshold gives a more accurate profile of student learning than verifying retention of knowledge.

Student Reaction to Learning Thresholds

We interviewed students about discovering learning thresholds, and we heard statements like this: "I now realize when I really have something down, and it makes me feel great. But it also shows me I really may not know something that

I thought I knew, and wow, I need to go back and learn it. But that going back is motivating and personal instead of something that I was told to do."

Another student remarked, "When I know my limit and the expectations, information comes into my focus, and I am better able to admit quickly that it is something within my limit and something I can handle on my own. Or, I realize that the expectation is not within my grasp, and I need to research, listen, or collaborate with a partner."

When students confront their threshold, they will be more honest with how they must approach new learning and growth. Likewise, students are more accepting of honest feedback when they know they are near their learning threshold. Moreover, they will have increased motivation and satisfaction, as they create more transferrable learning skills. Once a student establishes his or her learning threshold, there is potential for a more personal and rewarding academic experience.

Insight 2: Assessment Does Not Verify Learning; It Supports It

There are many aha! moments during the insight stage of team learning of proficiency-based assessment. One of the more exciting insights to emerge among a team of teachers is the realization that assessment actually *affects* learning—not just measures it. A great term from John Hattie (2012) that supports this idea is "assessment as feedback" (p. 141). Hattie advocates that the assessment itself should guide a student in learning. While some of us would like to think that we have always known this to be true, the reality is that our practices do not always align with this concept.

Dylan Wiliam (2011), in his text *Embedded Formative Assessment*, cites five elements that the Assessment Reform Group states must be in place for assessment to improve learning.

1. **The provision of effective feedback to students:** We contend that feedback must be viewed as an *echo* of student thinking, not as a product of teacher expertise. Feedback must provide students with guidance to find the quality in their own performance. In a proficiency-based learning environment, teachers achieve the correct feedback balance by teaching students to observe and identify thinking patterns and behaviors that translate to success prior to assessment, during instruction, and after the assessment.

2. **The active involvement of students in their own learning:** We are still shocked to find some teachers who don't teach students how to self-assess. Students in these classes are never held accountable to individualized learning and reflection. To fix this, reflection must be the

main learning task of each lesson—in fact, reflection is the hallmark of any quality lesson. If students are not held accountable to observe their own thinking patterns, then they will not trust their own self-assessing mind.

3. **The adjustment of teaching to take into account the results of assessment:** Simply put, students need an appropriate amount of time built in to lessons to react to feedback. Most lessons are planned for delivery of content and the action of engagement, not the involvement of assessment. Without thinking about how assessment works to support learning, reaction time will never be correct. It will be either too long or too short, causing learning to suffer. Instead, teachers must value and plan for how long it takes to digest the thinking that results not only from reviewing feedback but from the new thoughts that may be occurring during the lesson.

4. **The recognition of the profound influence assessment has on motivation and self-esteem of students, both of which are crucial influences on learning:** Students don't value feedback. When students do not value feedback as a learning tool, they become passive participants in their own learning, ultimately waiting for external catalysts to drive their learning, such as a teacher, the lesson, a formula, tutoring, or rote practice. All of these are external forces that act to demotivate students and lower the learning influence that their own thinking and reactions have. Quality lesson development includes more feedback interaction. Once students see the value in feedback, assessment has more potential to motivate. Think about an influential coach, mentor, or teacher you had in the past. Why was this person influential? It was most likely because you respected and valued his or her assessment of you, mainly due to the fact that the feedback you were getting was honest, open, and valuable. Lessons that include quality feedback exchanges not only encourage students to learn but also demand that students be capable of reflecting on their learning (Stiggins et al., 2004).

5. **The need for students to be able to assess themselves and understand how to improve:** Too many students reflect in isolation. When reflection is isolated to postassessment time frames, students will not see reflection as an engaging and important task. Likewise, neither will teachers. Reflection will be a checklist item that acts more as a ceremonial close to an assessment than a pedagogical tool. We must view reflection as engagement. Reflective engagement is most effective when it is done in relation to a well-composed proficiency-based target. The

teacher provides the reflective structure along with the proficiency-based target.

The idea that assessment supports learning is essential to proficiency-based assessment. Using assessment beyond simple verification of learning helps create learning environments that are more authentic, more meaningful, and more rewarding.

Insight 3: There Are Three Essential Elements of Teaching

As the team discovered in the story, when we sort through all the pedagogical tools, resources, activities, and theories, really only three elements are needed at any given time during the learning process (Wiliam, 2011).

1. Desired state

2. Current state

3. Gap thinking

All lessons must contain these three elements, and once they do, a teacher can draw closer to the effective implementation of proficiency-based assessment.

Desired State

The desired state, as outlined by countless practitioners including Wiliam (2011), is the *preferred outcome of learning*. Most teachers, upon hearing "desired state," scramble to create assessments and develop a new curriculum, leading to countless hours of reorganizing lessons, creating rubrics, seeking out new best practices, and attending workshops to hear about curriculum development. This can be a fruitless effort.

In proficiency-based assessment, the desired state *is* the proficiency-based target, not a means to accomplishing the target. As we stated earlier, in order for proficiency-based targets to be an effective target, they need to embody the expected state of competency. Traditionally, targets are viewed as specific, detailed, content-based, or action-based statements that simply organize learning. Proficiency-based assessment states that targets are much more than that—they are the expectation of the teacher. If we continue to view targets as something other than desired states, learning will be slowed or even stalled.

Current State

The current state refers to the student's awareness of his or her present understanding or application of a skill or topic. Some view a student's current state as something that needs to be graded and verified. But there is a twist here in proficiency-based assessment. Within proficiency-based lessons, we must *teach with* the current state, not simply *verify* it. What proficiency-based assessment dictates is that a student's current state is the material for the lesson. So instead of worksheets, activities, and so on, lessons are more effective if students produce a current state of understanding and subsequently refer to it during the lesson. A current state can be anything: an actual statement of where students think they are in their learning, a completed worksheet, a performance, a conversation, or even a thought. It doesn't matter what shape it takes; the student simply needs to be made aware of it during each lesson. This awareness of current states is crucial to learning, so, as teachers, we must work to capture students' current states early and often!

Gap Thinking

Many teachers do a decent job with the prior two elements; however, it is this third element that causes an issue and with it brings the biggest misconception: fix the deficiency and you will achieve a desired outcome. Deficiency models of learning are common and have the potential to force the lesson to reflect an outcomes model. This is due to the gap being interpreted as *what the student does not know* instead of as *emerging proficiencies*. We would be better off looking at the quality of the student's thinking inside the gap between the desired state and current state of the student, instead of at the gap itself.

Proficiency-based learning refers to this idea as *capturing gap thinking* (Wiliam, 2011). Gap thinking is the patterns of thought that are illuminated as students attempt to distinguish between their *current state* and a *desired state*. Different from gap deficiency, which is the reason or reasons why a student's current state isn't a desired state, gap thinking is what the students articulate or demonstrate while attempting to turn their current state into the desired state. To highlight this point, take the following two scenarios. The first represents a focus on a gap deficiency, and the second represents gap thinking.

- **Scenario 1:** A parent observes a child attempting to ride a bike, and the child is continually using his feet on the ground to brake. This deficiency-focused parent does not focus on why the rider thinks that is the method to brake but instead immediately tells the rider to use the foot brake and asks him to ride on.

- **Scenario 2:** A parent observes the same child but attempts to gain insight into why the child is using his feet to brake instead of the foot or hand brake. Ultimately, the reason the child is foot braking could be due to many reasons: it's fun, the pedal brake is broken, he doesn't know how to pedal brake, it helps him balance better, he didn't know there was a foot brake, he didn't know there was a hand brake, and so on.

If a teacher acts in the way the deficiency-based parent did in scenario 1, he or she would simply skip over the current state of understanding in order to expedite the remediation process. However, if a teacher follows the act of the gap-thinking parent in the second scenario and attempts to uncover the child's perspective of his current state of understanding, it exposes faulty logic, misconceptions, reflective thinking, and so on. Capturing, reviewing, and providing feedback on the quality of the student's thinking is far more effective at producing growth than capturing, reviewing, and providing feedback on the student's deficits. This practice of gap thinking leads to better feedback and ultimately leads to faster application of new learning.

Insight 4: The Three Essential Questions of Assessment for Learning Have Deeper Corollary Questions

Stiggins et al. (2004) outline three questions of assessment *for* learning, as follows.

1. Where am I going?

2. Where am I now?

3. How can I close the gap?

This is an effective tool to frame and guide lessons (Stiggins et al., 2004), but we have also seen these questions implemented incorrectly to create an experience for students that is not conducive to growth and learning, but rather focuses on results and indicators of achievement.

Unfortunately, lack of clarity of these questions can create misunderstandings or misapplications of principles that they evoke. The misunderstandings are outlined in the following sections.

Where Am I Going?

This is the primary question that all students must ask themselves when they are learning. The problem is that this question can create an outcomes-based experience and send teachers into product-based assessment implementation. Students will ultimately work to satisfy the teacher's exemplars and reach for an outcome, instead of focusing on their learning needs and growth.

In order to avoid misapplying the question and focusing on outcomes, we propose framing the question as "How well do I need to know or learn it?" This question places the focus on proficiency instead of outcome. By asking this question, students are very aware of the expected quality. When the essential element of the desired state (noted in insight 3) is clear, students have the information they need to answer this question.

Where Am I Now?

This question again tends to create a product-based assessment environment because it invites teachers to verify student outcomes and encourages students to strive for outcomes. Since students are reliant on the teacher for verification of their learning and feedback, they don't focus on becoming self-assessors. Similar to the "Where am I going?" question, "Where am I now?" also benefits from adjustments that focus on *how well*. The alternative question, "How well am I doing?" brings the teacher's expectation of competency into the core of planning, instruction, assessment, and learning and encourages a student's self-reflection. A student can successfully answer this question by reflecting on a proficiency-based target as it relates to their current state of understanding. A student can use the proficiency language of the target to create a learning perspective that is more accurate. While the question "Where am I now?" is often misinterpreted as "I know the material or I don't," the question "How well am I doing?" encourages students to distinguish between their work and what is expected of them, suggesting that learning is a dynamic process and not a static series of results.

How Can I Close the Gap?

This question is probably the most underthought and misunderstood of the three. Ultimately, this question takes learning accountability away from development and places it on deficiency. When we struggle to think about learning in context of a gradation, students default to a remediation model of self-assessment: "I have gaps in my learning, and I must fix the gaps to learn. I must practice and practice some more." In proficiency-based assessment, we believe that deficits are not the issue, and closing the gap means that students must discover what thinking got them in trouble in the first place. They are better able to make such discoveries by asking, "What will I be able to do if I do or don't know it?" This question not only suggests the idea of a flexible learning environment but also balances the accountability of learning between student and teacher in a healthier way. Students are now accountable to make sense of their own thought patterns and begin to value their own thinking as a learning tool, and the teacher is responsible for creating lessons that allow the students the time and space to do so. Shifting the focus to this question provides students with the metacognitive experience that is essential to the learning process, and it asks the teacher to develop lessons based on a gradation of proficiency. When the essential element of gap thinking (featured in insight 3) is embraced in the classroom, students are able to focus on their thinking instead of just attempting to arrive at the right answer. Table 4.1 illustrates the alignment of the assessment for learning questions and the proficiency-based corollary questions.

Table 4.1: Alignment of Assessment for Learning Questions to Proficiency-Based Assessment Essential Questions

Assessment for Learning Questions	Proficiency-Based Questions
Where am I going?	How well do I need to know it?
Where am I now?	How well am I doing?
How can I close the gap?	What will I be able to do if I am proficient? What will I be able to do if I am not?

While these questions have obviously proven to be extremely effective, proficiency-based assessment provides opportunities for teachers to dive deeper with these effective corollary questions, driving proficiency into the center of the instructional exchanges between teacher and student. These new questions refocus the original three by asking the students to make claims about what misunderstandings they may have had. The reflection results in self-prescriptive cures for the now uncovered misunderstandings.

Key Points

Following are key points from the chapter that readers should review to ensure they have a firm grasp on the content.

- As teams discuss proficiency-based assessment and reach insights, they will begin to see instruction differently. They are better able to incorporate the role and the worth of reflection in the learning process.

- In effective proficiency-based assessment, teachers focus on the desired state of learning, the current state of learning, and gaps in thinking.

- In proficiency-based assessment, questions to facilitate learning should be as follows: How well do students need to know or learn it? How will they learn it? What will they be able to do if they do or don't know it?

- The team leader ensures consistent understanding of proficiency-based learning within the interlocking roles of curriculum, instruction, and assessment; he or she frames the team's consensus around the insight.

Chapter 5

Evaluation

The evaluation phase is inherent in the work of a high-functioning collaborative team. At this point in our team's journey, the members have prepared themselves with guided professional development around approaching curriculum, instruction, and assessment differently. They have brainstormed, thought together, had their doubts, explored each other's viewpoints, considered setbacks, and rehashed. In other words, they've worked through the creative process, and now they've decided to move forward with their shared and agreed-on insights. As a high-functioning collaborative team, they've come to decisions they believe will help student learning and facilitate continuous growth.

That's all good. But the creative train should not stop there. Creativity demands evaluation and judgment. And, yes, you can definitely say that our team has been judging ideas quite a bit during the first three phases of the process. The creative process is recursive in that manner. The evaluation phase is more intentional. It is concentrated and focused on determining whether the insight or creative choice is a winner or a loser or somewhere in between. This is the phase of the process when the creative choice is up for critique, and a metric is set to help determine the effect of the change effort.

Evaluating a new change in practice is essential to our work with students. We must be constructively critical about the work we are doing, and we must have ways of knowing how and why a change is working or not working. During the creative process, it is important to build the evaluation tool prior to instituting the change. The team can reflect on the questions: What will indicate that we know we are doing better? Will it be data? A survey to gather feedback? Whatever the evaluation tool might be, make sure that you can gather information quickly and that you can react to the data in real time. Make sure that your evaluation methods are strong enough that you can correlate the data to the instituted change. For instance, can a common formative assessment help your team better understand the effectiveness of a lesson?

Following are three key points to remember during the evaluation phase.

1. Collaborative teams practice deep, intentional collective inquiry. The evaluation phase is data driven and offers specific clarity around whether the implemented change is effective.

2. This is a point where the team slows down and reflects. It is important to not jump to conclusions. The better team considers multiple angles to evaluation.

3. Leadership is about encouragement and asking the right discerning questions. Don't forget to celebrate successes and identify those successes, too—even if they are small wins. Likewise, the evaluation of the data might bounce team conversations back to the preparation phase, to the incubation phase, or toward new insights. This is all a healthy sign of continuous improvement.

The team story that follows illustrates the evaluation process at work. Notice how the creative process is questioned and how continuous understanding and growth are nurtured among the team. These types of open, honest, evaluative dialogues are significant to the mindset of teachers who want to constantly learn, try new and better efforts, and break teaching and learning patterns that are not effective. As you read our team's story, pay attention to the following three challenges.

1. As a team, teachers challenge themselves to evaluate not only the student data but also the effectiveness of their instruction.

2. In proficiency-based assessment, evaluation is different—the data must reflect *how well* students demonstrate what they know, understand, and can do, *not* just whether they know it.

3. During the evaluation phase, teacher leaders must challenge the team to identify and prove student learning and growth.

Our Team's Story

Over the next few weeks, the team felt more confident about evaluating its efforts to work with the practices of proficiency-based assessment. Team members were eager to reflect on the way targets and assessments were now being used as instructional tools, and they were curious to know what their colleagues were now thinking. When they last met, everyone shared his or her insights, but now team members were interested to know if those insights helped to improve teaching and learning. As a norm, they agreed to be open to sharing both their successes and failures. They all trusted one another, and they were all committed to helping each other when they confronted challenges throughout the year. For this team, one of the benefits of working with proficiency-based assessments was the ongoing discussion about student learning.

As the meeting began, Bruce noticed the members' heightened energy and enthusiasm. From a number of positive informal discussions with his colleagues, the new insights sounded meaningful and purposeful. Bruce started the meeting, saying, "Wow, it sounds like we are ready to think about how we are evaluating our practices as we work with proficiency-based assessment. The purpose of today's discussion is to consider the data we are collecting related to our work and to evaluate our successes or setbacks. Nothing is ever perfect the first time, so let's highlight our norm that we can trust one another to share both strengths and weaknesses as we've worked toward integrating our newer viewpoints around the function of assessment. As we are working today, we will also spend some time creating a way to evaluate our work more formally as a team."

Morrison added, "I never thought I'd say this, but I feel this initiative is gaining some traction. I like the way we are collaborating and creating a shared understanding as we are working together. Let's continue moving forward!"

With that, Bruce outlined the unit in which the team would be attempting to implement targeted gradations of proficiency and proficiency-based assessment.

He discussed the protocols of proper lesson study, reviewed the lesson the team had created in the prior meeting, and discussed the time line for implementation, as well as the data-collection process. Bruce and the team recognized that they were now evaluating their new insights into proficiency-based assessment as if they were doing collaborative action research.

Once Bruce was finished, he asked the team members how they felt, and they all agreed they were ready. With that, Bruce ended the meeting and reminded them that they would discuss the findings in depth at their meeting the following month.

Bruce and the team tested the proficiency-based assessment principles multiple times throughout the unit and made some good discoveries, and he and his colleagues observed each other and how they were implementing the skills the team had discussed. In doing this, they collaborated in a way that increased their shared understanding and support of one another's work. They were implementing that shared commitment to proficiency-based assessment, and they were enthusiastic to meet up as a group to debrief the results.

When the team got back together almost a month later, everyone had a lot to say. Bruce started, "Good morning. I hope you all found the last few weeks insightful and rewarding as much as you may have found it a challenge. When we met last, we reviewed the three major elements of proficiency-based assessment: (1) proficiency-based targets, (2) proficiency-based instruction, and (3) proficiency-based reflection. These elements create a clear vision for where learning is headed, provide tools to determine if the teacher or students have lost their way, and produce lessons of perpetual instructional change. They not only support quality instruction and curriculum but, more importantly, create rigorous and equitable assessments that align with a proficiency expectation."

Bruce handed out note cards and continued, "Let's first discuss the target element and our biggest realizations about proficiency-based targets. Write those on the front of the card; on the back of the card, write down any questions that still linger."

The team members took a good amount of time to reflect on their experiences over the last month and completed both sides of the cards. When they were finished, Bruce collected the cards, neatly organized them in front of him on his desk, and began the next part of the meeting.

He started, "I would like to use the words on these cards to frame our discussion. I know you all have a lot to share, but I would like to focus our conversation so that we can hear facts instead of opinions. Let's begin."

Vaughn, very proud of what she was about to say, jumped in, "Well, I made this nice review sheet that has several components. At the end of each day, I have students self-rank their learning growth against the gradation target. The students then look at their ranking on each target and explain why they are there and what they need to do to change it. Finally, they list all the resources that will help them get to the next level."

Britney asked, "Is it for points?"

Vaughn said, "No, it is simply for reflection."

Morrison added, "You do this every day?"

Vaughn said, "Yes. I feel that this practice helps my students understand where they are at and what they need to improve on. I don't even collect it."

Britney exclaimed, "Wow, that is amazing! Can I have a copy?"

Vaughn responded, "Sure! I will copy it for the whole team. I can show you next meeting how I do it."

Joni wasn't so sure and asked, "So how do you know where the students are at?"

Vaughn explained, "I collect the sheets before the review day for the test and look for patterns in the answers to help shape the review day. It helps me to build my lessons around what students say they know and don't know."

Morrison asked, "Do all students do it? What kind of answers do you get?"

Vaughn provided a good example and said, "I'd say my students answer it honestly and fully, and if they don't I can tell if they are struggling to reflect. For instance, the other day I spoke with a student who reported she felt very confident about the skills, but when it came time for the formative assessment, she didn't do well. That was an important conversation to have with her, and we were able to better identify where she needed to focus on improvement."

Joni said, "I like how it focuses in on students taking responsibility for their own learning, too. This fosters their responsibility to help each other, to better learn the material, and to gain multiple viewpoints."

Morrison asked, "OK, so besides reflecting on the targets, how did everyone instruct with these new targets, and did you find it useful?"

Britney spoke up, "I realized that by utilizing proficiency-based targets, students are now aware of what they know and how well they know it. It sounds like Vaughn and I are working with the same focus."

Morrison added, "I am not sure, but I think I understand. If students have an expectation of proficiency, then they can understand where their work is in relation to it. They don't need me to tell them necessarily."

Bruce smiled and added, "Yes. It seemed that my students suddenly became more accepting of my feedback too, simply because they understood where they stood relative to the expected level of work."

Joni said, "I felt my students allowed me to be more honest with them because they already knew where they were in relation to the expectation."

Bruce then added, "By utilizing targets in this manner students can now distinguish their own proficiency and the proficiency expected by the teacher—that's very different from our past practices." He paused. And then he continued, "Sure, students need a clear learning destination, but without the levels of competency radiating outward from that destination, students simply cannot identify their relative learning position. When this happens, instruction simply loses the ability to move learning forward."

Joni emphasized, "Those last few statements are important for us to remember."

Bruce pushed the meeting to another level by sharing a thought that he had been having over the last weeks: "Did anyone else notice that their classroom lessons demanded a lot more reflection?"

Britney responded, "Yes. One of the activities I tried was to have students rate themselves after completing each question on an assessment. I believe this is an old activity called GUS, in which students state after each question whether they *guessed*, were *unsure*, or were *sure*." She continued, "This really helped students make more sense of their performance on an assessment when they reviewed the correct answers."

Morrison challenged a bit, "Didn't that make the assessments really long? An extra question for each question?"

Britney agreed, "Well, yes, but I was wondering if our assessments needed to be so summative and so long. Can we have shorter, more meaningful assessments?"

Bruce inquired, "Are you suggesting that we make most if not all of our assessments formative?"

Britney, a bit cautious, said, "Well, yes—sort of. I don't know. I used to feel that to hold students accountable for their learning was to have a giant summative experience supported by a bunch of formative assessments."

After pausing a bit to gather her thoughts, she continued, "But now I feel that with these healthy targets, accountability and learning have transformed. I think that students need to learn to be excellent self-assessors, which is done with flexible and nimble assessments. These assessments then provide me as well as the students with timely evidence of their growth, and this is really all we need." Joni and Bruce added that they each had the same thought.

Morrison thought, "It seems that our previous targets led us to view assessment, reflection, and instruction as separate entities. But now, with our expectations acting as our targets, it appears that instruction and assessment are the same."

Bruce explained that he was no expert in this proficiency-based stuff yet, but said he had reread all the literature with a new lens and discovered several things. "First," he said, "I do agree that instruction and assessment are the same thing. And to go further, reflection is vitally important. I read in an article recently that said, 'Students, in all senses of the word, must learn to be adequate self-assessors of their own proficiency in relation to any expectation that is set before them.'"

Joni chimed in, "So that is what our new proficiency-based targets are allowing us to do."

Bruce continued, "Yes. The fundamental change in the way we view and write targets dramatically shifts our instruction and assessment to a more personalized reflective experience for our students, which is a more effective way to learn."

Continuing, Vaughn said, "This leads me to another point. I realized: assessment is not extracting answers from students but rather giving students the answers and allowing them to observe their thinking and decipher their reactions."

Britney identified quickly, "Our previous assessment efforts did not help students become, or develop the skills to become, excellent self-observers in the learning process. I'm learning that assessments don't just measure aptitude; they must measure the planning or thinking that the student employed to get the answer. That is where the real learning is, where the students' real knowledge lies—not in the production of the answer but rather in the preproduction of the answer."

Vaughn added something that she had read as well. "I read in my studies at school," she said, "that students are overconfident in their learning, meaning they cannot fully feel the limits of their knowledge. Often they think they know what they really don't know."

Bruce exclaimed, "Exactly! Why do we scaffold, why do we give summative assessments, and why do we constantly rewrite curriculum when all we really need are our well-written targets and the right instruction to reach those targets?"

Morrison noted, "And, of course, committing the effort into building the right instruction?"

Bruce said confidently, "Well, as I understand it now, in proficiency-based assessment the role of instruction is to help students value their own thought patterns and reflection as a learning tool. What I mean is, to be effective teachers we need quality learning targets and reflective spaces for students to engage with their own current understandings of those targets."

Britney said, "Can you give us an example? I need to understand this in the classroom setting."

Bruce decided to share his activity. "Well," he said, "over the last weeks, I had students compose a quick preassessment letter to themselves, stating in the letter what they expected to happen and why that would be the case. I urged them to stay away from simply writing items like 'I will get an A because I studied.'"

Bruce continued, "Instead, I instructed them to compose a letter that deconstructed the targets that were on the assessment. For example, 'Not only will I recognize the details of World War I, but I will produce all the main causes of World War I with clear details and will be able to connect the causes together through major events and people.' After they took the exam, the next day I handed back the letter and the exam and asked them to grade it themselves, then scrutinize their peers' work and ideas. Then, I gave the right answers to students and provided feedback. This was my lesson: reflecting about the assessment. Now I'm slowly realizing that all instruction should be reflecting on assessment."

Bruce finished with, "Remember the reverse 80–20 principle we talked about in our last meeting? We should spend 80 percent of our time on reflection and 20 percent on instruction."

The others chimed in with various questions as Bruce handed each of them articles to help achieve the reverse 80–20 principle in their classroom lessons.

Bruce, seeing they were low on time, added one last thing. "We have one more professional development day before the end of the year," he noted, "and I would like to continue our experimentation and discovery with proficiency-based learning. Please read these articles and continue to integrate new findings into your lessons, and gather all your observations for our next meeting. At this meeting, we can share our findings and continue improving in our practice."

The meeting ended in a great spot. All members were challenged not only by Bruce's questions but their own questions. The team reached a great new level of collaborative inquiry and wanted to ensure that all members were on a path to constantly refining their work in teaching and learning.

The Four Imperatives of Proficiency-Based Assessment

The evaluation phase is a period of time when teachers and teams evaluate their instruction and assessment efforts by paying close attention to student data. In this phase of our team's story, we see the team evaluating whether the new realizations uncovered in the insight phase are actually paying off for the learner. This can be challenging, as the team members must be both empirical in their thinking and continuous in their motivation to grow and learn from both successes and setbacks. It is during this phase that teams must decide if their insights were successful and if they had an impact on student learning. They must reflect on the worth of the insight on student learning or how they might need to elaborate on the insight to effect even greater, positive student growth.

During the evaluation phase of team learning, we see our collaborative team address four critical imperatives regarding proficiency-based assessment.

1. Provide students with ample opportunities and time to reflect.

2. Create strong learners.

3. Shift assessments from a verifying tool to a learning tool.

4. Create proficiency-based accountability.

Imperative 1: Provide Students With Ample Opportunities and Time to Reflect

Most educators would agree that reflection is an essential element of the learning process. Reflection involves many things, but first and foremost, it supports students as they learn more about themselves as learners. Reflective practice allows students to identify mistakes and self-correct any thinking patterns or processes that may have been off the mark (Stiggins et al., 2004). Without reflection, teachers and students cannot look back on the learning process and discern which thoughts or thought patterns or processes worked well for them and which didn't.

A major pitfall of the traditional model of instruction is that there are not enough opportunities for students to reflect; moreover, when they are asked to reflect, students may not be given enough time to fully develop those reflections. There is one major reason why this happens: reflective spaces are seen as *separate* from instruction and lessons.

It is difficult for some teachers to understand their role without thinking of themselves as *presenters* of knowledge. In proficiency-based assessment, teachers begin to see themselves as *mirrors* of knowledge, not the *presenters* of it. As long as teachers view themselves as presenters of knowledge, they will continue to see assessment and instruction as two separate entities.

A presenter mindset can create the teaching habits of (1) delivering content, (2) using assessments to verify that content was delivered to students properly, and (3) assigning feedback or a reward based on level of learning.

But remember, our charge as educators is to seamlessly connect curriculum, instruction, and assessment. Since the presenter's mind rarely pedagogically connects these entities, a constant shifting from one segment to another takes valuable time away from learning, and this thinking silently reinforces that learning must take place during the delivery of content.

Proficiency-based assessment suggests that learning happens when the students see and diagnose their own performance during purposeful reflective periods (Stiggins, 2001b). As we know from many experts, reflecting is learning—period. Without a reflective experience, learning simply doesn't occur (Schoemaker, 2011).

Proficiency-based assessment asserts that most students do not practice this naturally, so we must hold them accountable to these activities. If we don't hold students accountable, then we simply can't expect them to see their own growth. To help students develop this skill, we can build in reflective opportunities by asking students to do the following (Elbaum & Reibel, 2015).

- **Not only evaluate their work but also their thinking:** An example of this might be having students act against their own views to challenge their approach to a problem.

- **Scrutinize their own work publicly and relate their work or thinking to their peers:** An example of this may be asking peers to test students' thinking about their own work.

- **Examine their work and thinking in a variety of contexts:** An example of this may be having students articulate several approaches to a problem and then ask them to choose the one that has the highest potential to get the right answer.

We know from assessment experts that teachers should focus on formative assessment and help students become excellent self-assessors (Stiggins et al., 2004). These strategies will help hold students accountable and also provide the time and space to reflect, thus increasing its importance in the eyes of the student.

Embedding Reflection Into Instructional Practice

We've found that in many classrooms, 80 percent of the time is spent on instruction and assessing and 20 percent on reflecting. When teachers focus on proficiency-based assessment, their classrooms flip reflection to 80 percent, leaving instruction and assessing at 20 percent, fulfilling the reverse 80–20 principle our team discussed.

Let's see how this works.

In a linear model, it is difficult to provide ample time for reflection or self-observation due to the heavy focus on segmented success. However, proficiency-based assessment calls on teachers to concentrate on the inherent value that reflection brings to learning and the increased learning value when reflection is done in the presence of a proficiency-based target.

In this proficiency-based model, the proficiency-based target acts as the driving force of the lesson. The students then observe, review, and reflect on their formative assessments and draw closer to the expectation through reperformance (Wiliam, 2011). To make this model work, the teacher simply has the responsibility of doing two things: (1) constantly clarifying the proficiency-based target based on student evidence and (2) creating reflective structures for students to work within. Since the teacher is clarifying his or her expectation and simultaneously allowing time for students to see themselves in that expectation, lessons become more reflective. In fact, learning now depends on it.

Proficiency-based assessment outlines multiple ways to ensure that this reflective flip happens and a more contemplative environment is created (Moss & Brookhart, 2012).

- Identify which criteria are to be mobilized to meet the target.

- Teach with a proficiency-based target.

- Frame assignments as an opportunity to reflect objectively on an outcome, not to achieve the outcome itself.

- Provide an opportunity for students to capture and analyze their thinking during any task.

- Have students produce representative evidence and defend it using proficiency-based reasoning.

- Provide opportunities for students to take ownership of the criteria associated with good and bad thinking.

- Give students multiple opportunities to assess their own work in relation to the target.

A proficiency-based assessment model asserts that students reflect on every action and every decision they take or make in a classroom. As teachers, we must trust that new insights from gained reflective practices have potential for enormous cumulative benefits, far more benefits than our instruction.

Imperative 2: Create Strong Learners

When teachers ask students to constantly review and act on their current state of learning, students can potentially become frustrated and even exhausted. This happens because students either don't know how to use their current state of learning to grow or don't have the stamina to learn from it often. Since proficiency-based learning places a larger accountability on the learner, the reality is most students simply don't have the cognitive confidence and endurance to manage this landscape (Stiggins, 2001a). As teachers, we must determine whether our instruction creates the mental muscle our students need to be strong learners and survive in a highly reflective environment (Wormeli, 2014). In his book *How Children Succeed: Grit, Curiosity, and the Hidden Power of Character*, Paul Tough (2012) states,

> What matters most in a child's development, they say, is not how much information we can stuff into her brain in the first few years. What matters instead, is whether we are able to help her develop a very different set of qualities, a list that includes persistence, self-control, curiosity, conscientiousness, grit and self-confidence. (p. 30)

In proficiency-based assessment, we teach this set of qualities to create what is known as *learning durability*.

What Is Learning Durability?

We define learning durability as the ability to endure the demands of the learning process while sustaining a desirable level of competency (Tough, 2012; Wormeli, 2014). This durability increases a student's capacity to get more done, achieve more rigorous goals, increase his or her rate of learning, and increase effective self-reflections and engagement. In other words, with learning durability, learning becomes sustainable.

Why Is Learning Durability Important?

Learning durability is important for many reasons, but none is more important than *increased feedback acceptance*. Feedback acceptance can be defined as a student's willingness to internalize or apply the feedback for future learning (Bell & Arthur, 2008). When we observe classrooms and assessment processes, we find that feedback acceptance by students is shockingly low. To make the matter worse, in an attempt to increase the frequency of formative assessment, teachers are dedicating more instructional time to using this feedback. So more time is being dedicated to an area that students don't even trust!

Increasing feedback acceptance starts with being more honest with students. Current scaffolded lessons constantly safeguard against failure, and teachers must fight against low student learning stamina and accept the flaws of an outcomes-based culture (Schoemaker, 2011). Since teachers are creating lessons that are scaffolded to ensure success, feedback has a tendency to be safe, to be devoid of action-based language, and to lack a relation to the targeted proficiency (Wiliam, 2011). This lack of meaningful feedback causes students to silently reject the feedback given to them, seeing it as insignificant to their learning. As we've noted previously, students tend to rationalize the feedback more than accept and act on it (Schoemaker, 2011). Without the presence of a proficiency-based target, students tend to blame other factors for their deficiency when reviewing feedback and thus will have a skewed vision of their learning and abilities.

Since feedback in a proficiency-based environment is more purposeful, teachers must prepare students to endure and survive this honest feedback. A student can learn something, but it doesn't mean that it is going to stay learned in a new context or even stay with the student in the long term. For something to stay learned, students need to build the mental muscle—or durability—to keep it that way.

Why Is Learning Durability Hard to Build?

Teachers continually invest time in developing skills, knowledge, and competence. However, few of us build and sustain students' endurance to learn. Countless planning, instruction, and assessment hours may increase the volume of what students know and can do, but they often do not build the stamina to learn. There are several factors that make this durability difficult to build.

Student Pressures

Students feel overwhelmed by managing classwork, their calendars, and social pressures. In other words, the day-to-day demands of school are so overwhelming that learning is secondary. Students have no way of managing the tasks of the classroom and demands of school effectively, which forces them to demonstrate quick bursts of brilliance instead of focusing on long-term proficiency.

Teacher Pressures

Teachers are under many pressures while teaching: best-practice use, pressures from colleagues and leaders, planning time, and the expectation to constantly be analyzing and implementing new products and textbook resources, not to mention balancing their own professional learning. These current pressures cause an all-at-once approach to teaching, where teachers must toggle quickly between *all* components of education—teaching, assessing, and reflecting—to ensure that they have covered it all.

With all these duties that teachers must perform as well as the benchmarks they must hit professionally, it is no wonder why simplifying lessons into extremely digestible parts is the norm. This ease of simplification is the major reason why learning durability is never created.

Lack of Opportunity to Practice

Simply put, many of us struggle to understand how to promote learning durability through instruction. Unfortunately, our training as educators forces a view that there is a systematically correct way to teach: instruction, assessment, and reflection. This approach to teaching causes the value of proficiency (targets) to be lessened or even sidelined. In the absence of targets, teachers look for heavily systematic methods of teaching as if there is a neatly packaged set of tools that will automatically create learning for every student.

How Can We Build Learning Durability Through Resilience Coaching?

Resilience coaching is a major strategy to building learning durability. Resilience coaching as it relates to education can be defined as helping students accept the reality of their performance in the context of growth through learning (Coutu, 2002). Resilience coaching is teaching students to value their own thinking and value it enough to learn from. The purpose of resilience coaching in proficiency-based assessment is to help build learning durability. This concept follows Schwartz and McCarthy's (2007) similar idea that there are three energies that one must manage to be more productive and, more important, to stay focused and persist: (1) emotional, (2), mental, and (3) environmental. When this concept is applied to teaching and learning, there are three durabilities students must develop in order to learn effectively, as follows.

1. **Emotional durability:** Endurance of action, reaction, and interaction

2. **Cognitive durability:** Endurance of concentration, focus, and presence

3. **Climate durability:** Endurance of the formative environment, activity, and engagement

Each of the types of learning durability needs to be built and cultivated by using proficiency-based assessments. Let's look at each one closely.

Emotional Durability

When students are able to take control of their emotional reactions to an assessment, performance will improve regardless of the stakes or pressure of the environment. This means that first and foremost the students need to be aware of how they feel about their own thinking or performance to gain confidence in the reality of their performance (Chappuis, 2009).

Second, they must see the impact of their own thinking as it is applied to situations, but a key element here is that they see this impact in the context of a proficiency-based target (Moss & Brookhart, 2012). Once they see their own thinking applied to a more challenging context, they must evaluate how it impacts their effectiveness.

To build emotional durability, teachers must allow for intermittent recovery of emotions. One way to do this is by enacting a retake process. When students have an opportunity to evaluate their initial emotions from the first assessment, they must be allowed to reapply their insights—meaning they become more confident in using their own thinking.

We must have students acknowledge for themselves and reveal to others how well they have learned to cope with adverse situations and challenging problems (Tough, 2012). When we as educators create proficiency-based environments where students can be emotionally honest about their performance, they will significantly increase student learning and achievement.

Cognitive Durability

For some students, engagement in the classroom is not only emotionally difficult but cognitively difficult as well. Each day, teachers employ a complicated web of activities, dialogues, and assessments that aim at capturing evidence through multiple vantage points. Most teachers employ hyper-engaging lessons that default to activities that engage the maximum amount of students in the maximum amount of content, just simply to cover everyone's bases. As teachers, we must move away from all-encompassing activities that create only short bursts of impact and move toward activities that have long-term leverage and effects. To build endurance of cognition, teachers must help students navigate their thinking, lessen the distracting elements of their lessons, and structure reflective pauses within each class period.

Climate Durability

Teachers have created so many versions of formative assessments that the students, as well as the teachers, can't connect a purpose of the assessment to a proficiency-based target (Black & Wiliam, 1998). To build durability of the *classroom*, students need to see a clear purpose to what they are doing. Only when students experience the purpose of formative assessments and see the reality of their performance in relation to the proficiency-based target will their endurance in the classroom grow.

Imperative 3: Shift Assessments From a Verifying Tool to a Learning Tool

One of the more significant problems in assessment is that most assessments verify one level of proficiency, and once students show that competency, they are deemed proficient or at the mastery level. Some see this as a valid practice because many of our current assessments are based on outcomes and don't line up with proficiency-based targets (Marzano, 2006). If we do not align assessments with our proficiency-based targets, then we ultimately assess students on only part of our expectation (Marzano, 2006), making our assessments more of a verifier of learning than a catalyst for learning.

Most current assessment practices engage reflective thinking *after the assessment*, which means that it occurs much too late in the learning process to be of any value to the learner. Furthermore, reflective thinking this late in the learning process has little to do with actual learning.

To compensate for late reflection, teachers tirelessly work to turn around exams for students to review. However, this is often a fruitless endeavor and will only yield more stress for the teacher (Wiliam, 2011). Instead of refining our pre- and postassessment reflection activities, proficiency-based assessment challenges teachers to look to the assessment itself to alleviate this issue. The fact that traditional assessment systems struggle to be more than just authenticators of learning leads to many missed opportunities to expose students' thinking *as they engage* in the assessment process.

Creating Assessments That Capture Thinking

Proficiency-based assessment asserts that the data that matter most come from the thinking that takes place *during* the assessment (Schoemaker, 2011). As we have seen for many years, reflection-based assessments are very effective, and this concept is at the heart of proficiency-based assessment. We call them *reflective assessments* (Stiggins et al., 2004).

Reflective assessments are events that assess students on the quality of their thinking rather than the answer (Schoemaker, 2011). These assessments require students to record their thinking during the assessment, state the thoughts that went into the questions, decide between several problem-solving strategies, and even decide how this question relates to all the others that have been asked (Chappuis, 2009). These data regarding students' thoughts allow the teacher to become more aware of student misconceptions and how those misconceptions developed.

Proficiency-based assessment teachers understand that discovering the origin of a misconception is more valuable in the assessment of a student than interpreting an outcome. The data that teachers receive from a reflective assessment help them design instruction that meets the real needs of students and more importantly provide the correct feedback that expedites the learning process.

Creating these types of assessments can be done in the following ways.

- **Use direct reflective questions:** Teacher includes reflective prompts for the student to answer on a question, segment of the assessment, or the assessment process itself. Some examples include—

    o What if I told you another cause of World War I was political fallout in Egypt? Would your answer be different? Explain.

    o What may be another way to approach this question?

    o What was the first thing you noticed about this problem?

    o What was the crucial part of the process you used to solve the problem?

- **Use reflective pauses:** Teachers can embed reflective pauses within the assessment to gain insight about the student's confidence levels, process thinking, patterns of thinking, and so on.

For example, the teacher can include a pause in an exam and ask the student to reflect on whether she or he is ready to go on to the next section. This gives the student a chance to think about her or his current state of learning and also gives the teacher the much-needed context for any errors a student will make. For example, if the student says she or he is ready to go on but then misses all the questions, the teacher can use the context to create the appropriate intervention for the student.

- **Lessen the importance of outcomes:** Teachers can assess students on their quality of thinking as much as the quality of their answer by exploring the approach a student uses to arrive at an outcome rather than focusing on the outcome itself. This can be accomplished by grouping possible answers, showing the answer, and asking students to explain why other answers are wrong.

- **Use reflection logs:** Teachers can ask students to record their thinking directly into a journal as they engage with each segment of an assessment. This log is not simply reflection of why or why not one gets the right or wrong answer; rather, it will contain process thinking about how a student reacts to, approaches, and thinks through a question or task of an assessment.

Reasons for Using This Type of Assessment

Reflective assessments have several main advantages.

- They assess students' thoughts in relation to an expectation.
- They reflect *how well* students have learned, rather than *what* (Sandrock, 2011).
- They scrutinize connections between thought and performance.
- They make students aware of *why* they know something.

Proficiency-based assessment suggests that if students are reflective about the quality of their thought, in relation to a proficiency-based target, then salient learning is taking place. Remember, promoting the *right* thinking is more important for learning than simply promoting thinking.

Imperative 4: Create Proficiency-Based Accountability

It is much more satisfying to be right than wrong, is it not? So it should come as no surprise that school is built this way—to reward being right (Schoemaker, 2011)—and that any action or event that is not taking students to a distinct outcome would be deemed a waste of time. This is why reflection is often seen as unimportant—let alone *proficiency-based* reflection.

Furthermore, since some students may be indifferent about reflection, there will inherently be no accountability in the act of reflection. They may not even feel that reflection is meaningful or even essential to learning. If there is no accountability in a reflective process, students are allowed then to rationalize, distort, blame, and so on every time they receive feedback (Schoemaker, 2011). In this way, school is all smoke (lots of activity and action), but no mirrors (no accountability for reflection).

There are several reasons why students are not held accountable for reflection.

- The teacher doesn't outline a clear expectation of proficiency (Moss & Brookhart, 2012).

- Students do not know how to be good eyewitnesses to their own learning experience.

- Assessments are of poor quality and provide faulty evidence, meaning the assessment produces data that are not aligned to the gradation of learning (Marzano, 2006).

- The teacher feedback doesn't relate to a proficiency-based target and doesn't accurately capture what actually happened (Wiliam, 2011).

However, if reflection were effectively deployed in classrooms more, students would see its value and ultimately engage in its practice more readily. University of Maryland education professor Linda Valli (1997) outlines five types of reflection that are necessary for maximum effectiveness. We have adapted the five types and apply them to proficiency-based assessment, as follows.

1. **Collective reflection:** Reflective activities that analyze the learning experience as a whole

2. **Performance reflection:** Reflective activities that have the students review growth on all targets and performances

3. **Forward reflection:** Reflective activities that have students project or anticipate what they expect to happen (This reflective practice can be done prior to any assessment or performance.)

4. **Active reflection:** Reflective activities that allow students to record their own thinking and plan their approaches to problems as they are engaged in the assessment or learning event

5. **Conclusive reflection:** Reflective activities that allow students to draw conclusions about their performance, and most importantly, to judge their effectiveness as it relates to a proficiency-based target

Proficiency-based assessment states that to better serve our students, we want to create lessons that contain these types of reflection and that teaching and learning should center on the reflection. However, there is a twist. Reflection must center on a proficiency-based target. Without this, reflection is not as effective as it should be.

How to Hold Students Accountable for Reflecting

In proficiency-based assessment, we maintain that all new learning a student makes comes from a proficiency-based reflective experience, not from reflection alone (Schoemaker, 2011). Reflection without the presence of a proficiency-based target is just arbitrary and leads to shallow learning. If a teacher believes this statement like we do, then that teacher must hold the students accountable to the proficiency-based target.

In their article "Using Student-Involved Classroom Assessment to Close Achievement Gaps," Stiggins and Chappuis (2005) outline several strategies to hold students accountable for their learning.

- **Providing opportunities for self-assessment:** Teachers must allow multiple opportunities during each lesson for students to review their own work.

- **Pausing for classification:** Teachers must ask students to state what they perceive in their own work before placing their work on a rubric. Through this approach, students develop the skills to review their own work for patterns, tendencies, and other observable qualities that are related to the proficiency-based target.

- **Asking students to scrutinize their work and the work of others:** Teachers must provide opportunities for students to compare their current state of learning with others'. Each student using a set of criteria related to a proficiency-based target to evaluate each other's work can accomplish this.

- **Allowing students to revise their learning:** Teachers must structure lessons so that students have the opportunities to not only capture a current state of understanding but also allow them to revisit and amend that understanding amidst new information or context.

- **Having students record their thinking:** Teachers must provide students the opportunity to record their thinking process as they engage in activities and performances. This allows the student to review and observe the process they are using during the assessment event or lesson.

- **Having students plan ahead:** Teachers can ask students to develop an action plan for the activity or learning they are about to engage in or even generate anticipatory questions they may have before the event.

- **Having students reflect on the target:** Teachers must allow students the time to review feedback from the assessment in relation to the target. Without the presence of the target, the reflective process may seem arbitrary and pointless.

- **Providing formative reviews:** Teachers must allow students to review all the evidence that was collected for a particular target and use that evidence to set goals, annotate the evidence in the portfolio, and self-assess their current state of learning.

Why There Is No Proficiency Accountability

Since students don't naturally connect their own thinking and learning to a proficiency-based target, reflection doesn't make a whole lot of sense to them. Students caught up in the tasks or business (homework, summative exams, presentations, and so on) of the classroom can find themselves overwhelmed by the complexities of the content they are expected to master. This is often due to a focus on grades, a short-term focus of knowledge retention, and high-stakes testing. It is because of this business that reflection is minimized and even segregated from the learning process. Students simply don't see reflection as being as valuable as the logistics of learning.

If we don't help students reflect against an expected proficiency, then they will continue to rely on possible flawed knowledge foundations that may cause learning to feel disconnected, exhausting, and tedious and can lead to average success or even failure. With no proficiency-based reflection, students can potentially foster negative beliefs about their ability, which undermine confidence and motivation.

How to Create Proficiency Accountability

In proficiency-based environments, students record reflection *during* instruction and during assessments—students speculate on multiple approaches to learning content and scrutinize their thinking to ensure a more flexible and solid knowledge base. If teachers hold students accountable to reflect against a proficiency-based target— during instruction and during assessment—students gain a deeper perspective and increase their capacity for growth.

Proficiency-based accountability can be defined as ensuring that each student is engaged with his or her own thinking in the presence of a desired level of competency— all the time. This means reflection simply isn't meaningful if it is not done in the presence of a proficiency-based target.

A teacher can develop proficiency accountability through proficiency-based reflective instruction and student-centered formative assessment.

Proficiency-Based Reflective Instruction

Proficiency-based teachers desire to know one thing: what students think about their own current state of thinking. Proficiency-based assessment asks teachers to strive to understand *how* their students are thinking—not to focus on the outcomes of their learning or to simply verify their current state (Chappuis, 2009).

To practice proficiency-based reflective instruction, teachers must adopt the following mindsets (Marzano, 2009; Moss & Brookhart, 2012).

- Teachers must make students see reflection as complementary to their performance.

- Assessments should aim to capture thinking, clarify thoughts, and focus on development, not on outcomes.

- Teachers must develop all activities and strategies that associate with the proficiency language of the target.

- Teachers must instruct to help students think about how feedback relates to the target.

One way to apply these mindsets is to structure a formative assessment in ways that force reflective thinking. For example, a student could choose from the following options before the teacher reveals the correct answer (Chappuis, 2009).

- **Choose another student's answers:** Students who choose this option must state why they chose their peer's answer.

- **Use the teacher's answer, which may be right or wrong:** The teacher admits up front before the event that the answer he or she is showing is either right or wrong but does not say which.

- **Provide the most common answer from the last few years:** Historical relevance is entered into the activity for another perspective.

Which would you pick? These options can potentially not only make instruction and assessment the same entity but they lessen the outcome of getting the answers and increase the thinking environment. When thinking is alive in instruction, we allow reflection to act as the core of learning; students see more purpose in reflection, and teachers use reflection data to assess students more effectively. With an activity like this, rather than thinking of reflection as yet another task that is added to the lesson, students view it *as* the lesson. The emphasis is now on being a reflective learner rather than an achievement learner.

By injecting proficiency-based reflection into the classroom experience, teachers clarify the expectations for the students and in doing so outline the purpose of the formative assessments that will relate to this particular proficiency-based target (Moss & Brookhart, 2012). It is also important that teachers choose reflective activities that have a very clear purpose and a tangible relationship with the proficiency-based target. For example, consider the instructional segments of supporting explanations with effective examples, creating viable explanations, organizing explanations in a written analysis, and answering free-response questions for the target *Using examples from class, effectively explain the main political, economic, and social causes of World War I in a written analysis.*

Reflective proficiency instruction will provide your students with internal inquiry as part of their everyday learning. In this way, each experience in the classroom will contribute to their growth and learning.

Student-Centered Formative Assessment

In a teacher-centered classroom, learning passes through the teacher's gate and there is high potential for creating an outcomes-based environment. In these classrooms, students may struggle to develop self-reliance in the learning process and thus are unaware of their own thinking and ultimately don't trust it to learn (Chappuis, 2009). These classrooms are teacher centered. While most teachers have moved away from teacher-centered classrooms, some are still not creating the engagement that is needed for students to develop as self-aware learners. Even some of the most polished lessons simply don't allow students to perceive themselves as effective thinkers. Essentially, many teachers feel the need to see a student's aptitude instead of creating spaces for students to see their own aptitude and emerging proficiency. These spaces can be created through student-centered formative assessments (Popham, 2009).

Teachers can embrace student-centered formative assessments by simply allowing formatives to become student assessed, student managed, and reflected on by students. By giving this control to students, teachers will need to work hard to reframe misperceptions for their students. Students must be taught to embrace the learning potential of using formative assessments to self-observe and self-assess to develop competency (Stiggins et al., 2004).

Student-centered formative assessments (Popham, 2009) have a number of advantages, including the following that we have identified and adapted from Chappuis (2009) and Stiggins (2001a).

- They increase students' ability to self-assess and be self-aware.
- They help students find their learning threshold.

- They widen students' perspectives about themselves as learners.
- They create flexible and adaptive thinking skills.
- They help students develop trust in their thinking.

As educators, we must strive to value our students as thinkers. We must model to them that their thoughts are valued and have the potential to create a quality learning experience for them. By creating student-centered formative assessments, students can become what Schoemaker (2011) calls *forensic learners* who "learn to recognize their own cognitive blind spots, tendencies such as wishful thinking, overconfidence and selective perception" (p. 321).

Key Points

Following are key points from the chapter that readers should review to ensure they have a firm grasp on the content.

- During the evaluation phase, the team will seek continuous growth and improvement. In proficiency-based assessment, the team must readdress its initial goals and purposes for implementing a proficiency-based model. First, the team must evaluate the capacity of the assessment to measure the learning target. The assessment should provide students with the opportunity to demonstrate all that they know. Then, the team must evaluate the assessment to determine if it is written in a way that addresses these purposes.
- The evaluation phase needs to include a team discussion about instruction. Based on the assessment data, the team should review the strengths and weaknesses of the instruction that led up to the assessment. The team members should determine the value of their instructional choice for the learner.
- The evaluation phase reviews students' reflective thinking and perceptions of learning growth. The team should review whether students were confident in their thinking as they completed the assessment; this discussion should affect future instructional choices.

Chapter 6

Elaboration

Developing individual and collaborative team mindsets that embrace continuous growth and improvement is key to ensuring students' success and developing their potential. However, at some point, team members start to ask, "When is good just good enough? Can't we just leave it all alone this year?" The point of our work, though, is to move our instruction—and our schools—forward. Our responsibility is to lead a culture of continuous improvement and promote success for every student. This is a demanding responsibility, and it requires the capacity to elaborate on the good work we are doing to make it great and even greater. During the creative process, *elaboration* means to build up an idea, tinker with it, nuance it, and develop the idea's fuller potential. Elaboration is the immediate response to evaluation. At the evaluation phase, the team questioned how well the new idea worked, noticed patterns and trends in data, and identified the degree to which the idea was a winner or a loser. Here at the elaboration phase, the team is responsible for making needed adjustments toward improvement.

The elaboration phase is an ongoing and thriving process of collective inquiry. As we've seen the team develop through each phase, we want to restate that the creative process is not linear or formulaic. The elaboration phase is a rich example of this dimension of the creative process. Individuals and teams will likely dip back into preparation. For instance, they might want to review previous learning or explore more sophisticated understandings. They might slow down and incubate ideas after evaluation. They will certainly develop insights.

Following are three key points to remember during the elaboration phase.

1. This phase is about continuous improvement. Elaboration can be about fine-tuning, nuancing, or evolving a change.

2. During this phase, the team sees the value of the change and wants to build on it. The team members are now ready to serve as teacher leaders, sharing their struggles and success with other teacher teams.

3. At this point, the leader supports the value of continuous improvement and the values around success for every student. The leader might ask, "Is this change working for every student or subgroup of students? How so? If not, how might the change be more beneficial for more learners?"

When reading about our team's journey, consider how the entire creative process seems to be at play now. Identify how the team builds up an idea in a way that makes it better. Ask, "How are team members elaborating on the good work they are already doing?" As you read our team's story, pay attention to the following challenges.

- The team members are challenged to identify how they can continuously improve their work with students. They should refer back to the evaluation phase to consider these elaborations to their work.

- The team should identify small changes that can better differentiate instruction for all students; however, that is often not enough. The team members should, when necessary, consider the evolution of their instructional choices that go beyond tweaking small details.

- The team leader helps celebrate the successes and the further developments of the team. He or she retraces the strengths of the team's decision-making patterns and continues to replicate and build off this pattern. In this way, the team leader continues to foster mindsets toward continuous improvement.

Our Team's Story

One of the overriding efforts during the evaluation phase was to review and examine results. Bruce's team knew that results were sometimes positive and sometimes very disappointing. The team norm was to learn from results and make revisions to teaching and learning in a way that fostered continuous improvement. At this point, team members operated with a mindset that they all enjoyed—where ideas and insights were constantly emerging in relation to new learning. Instead of looking at change as a series of disruptive shifts and turns, they viewed change to be constantly evolving to address the needs of students. They were monitoring and adjusting ideas in a way that fit the specific needs of their students, and they were finding ways to revise and approach teaching and learning differently for the needs of all students. In other words, they were elaborating on good ideas, nuancing them, and refining their curriculum and their instructional practices.

At this point, Bruce felt that within just one year his team had become a cohesive unit, moving learning and teaching forward unlike any team had done before. During the start of the next meeting, Bruce thanked his team. He began, "We have all worked so hard, and I am proud of our work and time together." The others quietly nodded toward one another in agreement. He asked each person to identify one point to celebrate about the work he or she had done—something that each team member thought was an impressive step forward. The group members went around the table, commenting on the strength and developed focus of their learning targets, the way they were better communicating about students, the small wins, and the ability to better identify ways to support student growth. They celebrated being collaborative and their willingness to explore better choices for students.

Bruce continued, "We need to begin thinking about the work we are doing and how we want to refine it. As we continue with our process to integrate proficiency-based assessment during the elaboration phase, let's commit to making good revisions based on our evaluation and new insights. I'd also like us to always consider any new learning we might need to do in order to develop our depth of understanding. I think this will help us to stay really engaged and creative with our work together. At this point, I'd like to discuss curriculum changes and some of the past concerns we've had about the scope and sequence of our curricular hierarchy. We've done a lot of work with scaling our targets. Let's compare how we've identified our targets and how we've articulated gradations of learning."

Joni spoke up. "Excuse me, Bruce," she said. "I don't mean to interrupt, but why do we still need this scope and sequence? Isn't the target hierarchy our curriculum already?"

The team members, including Bruce, reached to pull out the hierarchy of their targets.

Morrison spoke first. "Well," he said, "yes, I guess it really is. The only thing we really need to decide on is when or in which unit we are teaching each target. Or, more importantly, how long it will take before we have enough evidence on any given target."

Britney agreed, adding, "This hierarchy of targets is our curriculum, and what I like about it is that it's a curriculum that doesn't sit on the shelf; it's a curriculum that we are constantly discussing as a team."

Bruce thought out loud, "Well, OK then." He said, "I think you're right, and I'm excited to think about our curriculum in the way that Britney just said. It should be a constant, continuous discussion. The data from our results can help to lead our discussion toward decision making. For instance, can we pull out our assessments in unit 1?"

The team members pulled out the assessments and laid them on the table so all could see. Vaughn spoke before Bruce could outline what the team was even doing with the assessments. "Do we even need all of these assessments?" she asked.

Morrison said, "I would think so, but I will say this one," as he picked up one of the team's formative assessments, "is the best. I have used this assessment for a few years now, and there are none better at showing me how well students can demonstrate our learning targets."

Bruce spoke up, saying, "Yes, I think so too. It aligns with our new targets directly. We made this assessment without proficiency targets, but we—unknowingly— had proficiency at the center of our minds when we wrote this." He continued as he picked up the assessment. "If you look closely at it, with our new proficiency-based lens, you can see that it matches our scaled targets for this unit exactly. There are areas that collect evidence not of learning, but rather of *dynamic* learning."

"What do you mean by dynamic learning?" asked Vaughn.

Bruce described what he meant, "I mean that learning is dynamic, or ever changing. If you look at this assessment, we have many different sections of pre-proficiency and also extended-proficiency flanking the expected proficiency section. This setup helps us capture evidence of fluid learning taking place. If we are committed to every student, we need to nuance our instructional strategies so we help all of our students to proficiency. That way we can see how each student is attempting to move between each of the gradations in a learning target."

Britney laughed. "So in normal understandable terms, the assessment has the same structure as the target."

Bruce laughed too. "Yes," he agreed. "That would have been easier to say."

Morrison said, "Well, let's just use this one and scrap the rest."

The others sat and wondered for a moment. What if they didn't need all these assessments? What if they just needed that one?

Bruce said, speaking rhetorically, "What if it were the right assessment? Would we need more?"

After mulling over that question for a few moments, the team reviewed the assessment again. The team decided to create several modified versions of it and ended up with several assessments for the unit. All were scaled, and more impor-tantly, without even trying, all of the unit assessments became common formative assessments. All were collaboratively created and aligned to each gradation of the appropriate target.

As the members of the team sat quietly for a few moments after their assessment work ended, Joni said, "Now on to instruction—how are we teaching this unit?"

Bruce decided that they would dedicate the remaining hour to the topic of instruction, and how they might elaborate on their instructional practices so that they were reaching every student.

Vaughn spoke up, "I read something in proficiency-based assessment recently that helped me understand what instruction should be," she said. "If, like you said, Bruce, curriculum, instruction, and assessment are all the same thing—reflection— then the two crucial elements of instruction must be a proficiency-based target and reflective activities. But what does that mean? What happens in those reflective spaces, I wondered. And I read this: 'We must design lessons for mistakes and learning from mistakes.'"

She finished, "That, to me, means so many things, but what proficiency-based assessment says it means is we must build mistake tolerance in students."

Bruce jumped in, "That is interesting. Keep going, Vaughn."

Vaughn continued, "Well, with working with proficiency-based assessment, I realized how even the simplest lesson is complex and multivariable. Therefore, reflection is essential to learning. Without realizing this, I would have never bought into the whole reverse 80–20 principle. What we need to realize," she said, "is that lessons are entities that prepare the students' minds for great discovery. Therefore, we must plan systems of inquiry, not content delivery structures. That is how I began to change my lessons, building in intentional moments of reflection and inquiry."

Britney asked, "Did anyone start planning their lessons this way as well?"

Joni, after a few moments, raised her hand as she spoke. "I am not sure what you did, Vaughn," she said, "but I think I may be doing it as well."

Bruce nodded for her to continue.

"Well, all my formative assessments became my lessons. I would simply have the students work through the formatives, scrutinize their understanding and thoughts with their peers, compare their work to the target, and utilize timely feedback—all within the course of fifty minutes. There really wasn't much to it."

Britney challenged, "So you don't have any activities, just formative assessments?"

Joni quickly added, "But with all the work we have done with proficiency-based assessment, my activities have the target at the heart of them, thus making them formative assessments themselves—actually everything is now formative. I just gave the students more time to review their work against the targets. My students do a lot of comparing and contrasting their understanding against others'."

Bruce added, "So you are getting the students to observe and scrutinize their missteps and validate their successes—using these actions as the elements of your lesson?"

Joni said, "Yes. I use the students' interpretation of their own work as my lesson plan."

Morrison added, "This brings up something I've been thinking—the problem with current lessons is not that the students make too many mistakes; it's that they make too few."

Morrison continued, "If we scaffold our lessons so everyone 'gets it,' we actually bring learning to an impasse. These lessons produce high percentages of students who meet the target and there is little thinking, no reflection, no mistakes for the teacher to teach through. I think quality learning is about the dynamic relationship between the learner and their reflection."

Running short on time, Bruce tried to rally the troops to bring this home. Up to now, the team had finished unit 1's targets and had created all assessments and collected evidence for unit 1 as well, and it sounded like team members were close to an idea of how to instruct this.

Joni asked, "So how do we instruct then in this reflective style?"

Bruce, pulling the most recent article about proficiency-based assessment from his bag, said, "Well, we should think about it this way. Instead of reading this to you or having you read it too quickly, I will just highlight the instruction part of this article. It says there are five types of reflective instructional activities to plan for." Bruce showed the group the following list (Valli, 1997).

1. **Collective reflection:** Activities that reflect on the learning experience as a whole, having the students review growth on all targets and performances

2. **Forward reflection:** Activities that have students project or anticipate what they expect to happen (This can be done prior to a formative assessment or performance.)

3. **Active reflection:** Activities that employ functional thinking by the student (These activities allow students to observe their own thinking and plan their approaches to problems.)

4. **Conclusive reflection:** Activities that allow students to draw conclusions about their performance and most importantly to judge the effectiveness of their forward thinking and active reflection

5. **Performance reflection:** Activities that have the student review growth on all targets and performances

Bruce said, "I feel that these five types of reflective spaces are how we should plan all of our lessons . . . to accelerate learning. They will help us to elaborate on the good work we are doing."

Bruce continued, "We have a few minutes left, so why don't we take these reflective spaces and start elaborating our ideas around the instruction? Let's go back to the preparation phase and incubate our thinking again. Let's focus on what we might do differently as we make revisions."

The Four Realizations of Proficiency-Based Assessment

Even at the elaboration phase, it takes an incredible amount of energy and focus to maintain this level of practice. An elaborative practice moves at the same rate as experimental action and insightful reflection but is also a different experience altogether. At this point, ideas are being nuanced, or, in other cases, an evolution of thinking is taking place and extending an idea—maybe even completely.

While there is truly an infinite amount of emerging ideas that exist in the elaboration phase, the assertions developed throughout our team's journey that may potentially be the most impactful are the following.

- Assessments must capture more than outcomes.
- Formative assessment is for the student, not the teacher.
- Students must be active participants in the learning process.
- Feedback must be accepted.

While acknowledging these new assertions is an essential first step of this phase, our team must next commit to the idea that every assertion has high potential for nuance and extension. This is why it's called the *elaboration phase*. It is a stage where earlier learnings are stretched and nuanced in ways that lead to new insights into their practice. That is why the key to remaining in this stage is managing the new realizations that now exist due to the work throughout the other phases. This means that teams must maintain fidelity in their work but improve on that sturdy foundation through new insights into their learning. From our assertions on page 153 there are four new realizations we feel are important to focus on.

1. Students don't always use the same thinking during an assessment that they used when studying.

2. Errors can be informative.

3. Students must be active learners.

4. Teachers must avoid feedback distortion.

Realization 1: Students Don't Always Use the Same Thinking During an Assessment That They Used When Studying

Outcomes-based viewpoints don't tell a student's whole story; they lack nuances and fail to account for near misses or for good-enough answers. They also fail to account for the complexity of the world we live in and for the existence of external factors (Schoemaker, 2011).

If we take this perspective and apply it to the concept of assessment, we get an astonishing realization: a good portion of assessments are, in fact, outcomes based! These outcomes-based assessments tend to overlook the importance of student thinking and decisions made *during* an assessment. This is important because of one major fact: students tend to perform poorly not because of content deficits but rather because of ineffective decisions when applying that content (Schoemaker, 2011).

Let's put it this way. How many times have you heard a student state, "I got this," only to find out on the exam that he or she really didn't get it? This happens because the student really *did* get the content; it was in his or her brain, absorbed, so to speak, and ready to launch. However, the judgment the student used when employing that content during the assessment was flawed in some way. These ineffective decisions are the result of faulty thought patterns, which directly affect judgments (Schoemaker, 2011).

Committing to this idea will lead to the realization that assessment must capture more than outcomes. It must capture decisions and judgments that a student made to arrive at an outcome because, as we find, student reasoning in preparation for an assessment and when actually taking that assessment can differ. Why is this important to acknowledge? Mainly because it reveals two things.

1. Outcomes-based assessments are unreliable metrics to measure students.

2. Outcomes-based assessments are unreliable metrics to provide feedback.

Outcomes-Based Assessments Are Unreliable Metrics to Measure Students

Traditional assessments capture an outcome (answer) that is only representative of a student's absorbed knowledge prior to the exam, not the choices he or she made to arrive at the answer (Schoemaker, 2011). Far more students use in-the-moment decisions to answer questions rather than drawing from learned content or developed skill (Schoemaker, 2011). This is why outcomes (grades, percentages, and points) are unreliable and ultimately cloud the teacher's judgment of a student's proficiency.

In the following exercise we conducted, a group of 110 students was asked to complete a formative assessment. Students were asked to record responses to the following questions derived from Chappuis (2009).

1. Did you use the same thinking to answer the question here as you did when you studied?

2. Did you not know the answer at first, but new thinking emerged and you figured it out?

3. Did you guess or use random thoughts to answer the question?

These questions drive at the heart of formative learning and provide a more accurate view of student performance. We see the data from this scenario in table 6.1. In the first column, we have the percentage of students who answered correctly, and the subsequent columns list the number of students who chose each type of thinking.

Table 6.1: Intra-Assessment Reflection

	Percentage Correct	Used Same Thinking as When Studied	Did Not Know, but New Thinking Emerged	Guessed or Random Thinking
Question 1	91	85	11	4
Question 2	85	79	19	2
Question 3	81	55	28	17
Question 4	89	66	28	6
Question 5	57	53	36	11
Question 6	89	47	28	23

We can see in this scenario that the outcome itself, column 1, is an unreliable metric by which to measure students. It proves unreliable because it is simply far too shallow a view of how the students are learning the material. There is far too much context that surrounds an answer or result to take it at face value. To see evidence of this, just look at question 6. Only 47 percent of students answered that question on the exam with the same thinking that they used when they were studying!

An outcome (score, grade, or mark) that appears so solid in many educators' eyes actually has many underlying factors at play. As we look again at Schoemaker's (2011) work, he states, "Few plans survive contact with reality" (p. 393). We see the same thing happen in education. Students' thinking changes dramatically *as they take* the assessment, meaning that the thinking and knowledge that a student enters the assessment with are fundamentally different from the student's knowledge during and after the assessment. Often this happens because most students abandon their own thinking for what they think the test wants to hear or because new thinking emerges due to mounting insecurity or confidence, patterns of answered questions, or sudden inspirations.

So if simple-answer assessments are so obviously ineffective, why hasn't anyone fixed it already? Well, in teaching, it is far easier to capture aptitude than it is to capture thinking, planning, forethought, conceptions, misconceptions, or judgments (Schoemaker, 2011). Our current educational practice tends to sacrifice learning for the sake of systematic ease and preciseness. It is simple to just look at the outcome or an answer to assess who learners are. However, we must remember that while the answer is important, it is only the tip of the iceberg in understanding student learning.

As the example in table 6.1 (page 155) illustrates, students often veer from their prepared thinking far more than teachers know. The call of proficiency-based assessment is to assess how students' thinking changed direction as they completed each segment of the assessment. Furthermore, we are to ask ourselves, How well did that assessment capture the thinking or judgment that the students were utilizing as they answered the questions (Schoemaker, 2011; Stiggins et al., 2004)?

Outcomes-Based Assessments Are Unreliable Metrics to Provide Feedback

As we have described, our current educational system permits us to overlook hidden messages about how students learn. This permission makes it nearly impossible to accurately judge whether a student performed poorly or performed well, thus leaving grades inaccurate measures of student performance (Guskey & Jung, 2013). Even worse is that without uncovering these hidden elements (misconceptions, patterns of logic, and so on), feedback becomes inaccurate and almost meaningless in some cases, as we saw in the bike-riding example in chapter 4 (page 118).

Without addressing these obscured elements of student learning, how can teachers fairly judge student performance? How can they truly give accurate feedback and advice about a student? Most importantly, without uncovering these hidden elements of learning, a teacher's judgment of a particular student's performance will always be skewed, shallow, or inaccurate (Guskey & Jung, 2013). This skewed judgment of student performance can cause feedback distortion (Schoemaker, 2011) and allow students to distrust the feedback they receive. But there are ways to remedy this.

One method is by restructuring the way students interact with assessment. As John Hattie (2012) states in *Visible Learning for Teachers*, "An alternative is to consider 'assessment as feedback'" (p. 141). In order to fully benefit from the assessment process, students need to experience how the assessment itself provides feedback. Teachers must help them look at each assessment question through the lens of reflection, experiment with approaches to each question, and observe their thoughts while doing so.

One way to do this would be to include areas on assessment where students don't think about what the answer is, but rather explain the impact of the selections. Schoemaker (2011) defines this idea as *portfolio thinking*. Portfolio thinking asks us to look at problems not in isolation but in a collective group (Schoemaker, 2011). A teacher using this type of assessment model can ripen thinking environments so much that feedback and assessment have a clear purpose and connectedness.

For example, consider the following scenario in which a teacher originally had assessments that presented multiple-choice answers to a question and asked the student to choose one correct answer (such as in figure 6.1, page 158). Each possible answer was presented in isolation from the others thus forcing the participating student to focus on an answer instead of their process of thinking during the event. Now, however, she creates her assessments with portfolio thinking ideals by presenting the answers in pairs or groups (figure 6.2, page 158) and asking the students which group of answers was more correct, more incorrect, and so on, thus lessening the focus on an answer and instead inviting the participants to explore and record their thinking about the problem. The idea here is to eliminate the hunt for the right answer, which ultimately reduces the use of outcomes-based learning (Schoemaker, 2011). By grouping answers together and having the student defend both sets, a teacher can begin to see the students' thinking, mental processes, and judgments they may be mobilizing to learn. When this happens, a teacher can finally see *genuine* evidence of student learning.

Which graph represents the unemployment rate over the last eight years?

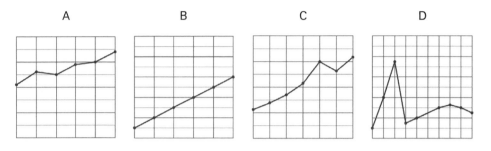

Figure 6.1: Traditional multiple-choice assessment.

Which group of graphs better represents the unemployment rate over the last eight years?

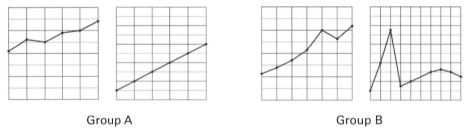

Figure 6.2: Proficiency-based multiple-choice assessment.

The idea of assessment is not for the student to tell the teacher what the right answers are, but what their thinking patterns are. One of the principles of proficiency-based assessment is that an assessment's purpose is not extracting answers from students but rather allowing them to observe their thinking and decipher their reactions (Stiggins, 2001a).

Realization 2: Errors Can Be Informative

To learn, students must make more mistakes than they deem optimal (Schoemaker, 2011). This means that students must err more than students like to err. This is very difficult to do—not just because students don't like failing, but also because teachers compromise this fact by *ensuring* that students don't. With lessons that are structured to avoid healthy dissonance and purposeful errors, students rarely have the opportunity to make mistakes, review them, and even learn from them.

Viewing education through Schoemaker's eyes, instruction needs to be centered on student-produced errors and reflection experiences that reveal misconceptions, competencies, and anything else that is related to student learning. Most learning typically accrues over the long run rather than being confirmed at the instant of the assessment—meaning that learning doesn't happen in a vacuum. Instead, learning comes from the continuous opportunity to perform actions that influence further thinking and action (Schoemaker, 2011). Proficiency-based assessment acts to ensure that students constantly view and experience this influence formatively. This occurs through formative assessment that is used *by* students, not *for* students.

Our current definition of formative assessment is taken from a teacher's perspective. As we stated earlier, a teacher, when asked about the purpose of formative assessment, will most likely say, "So *I* can know where students are in their learning." In a proficiency-based assessment model, the purpose of formative assessment is to help a student know where *he or she* is in his or her learning.

With proficiency-based assessment, formative assessments must be based on *proficiency-based targets*, which help students *assess their own* decision-making process. Formative assessments used by students clear out the brush of emotional reactions, logistical demands, and cognitive white noise. This use of formative assessment aims to solidify the learning process by destroying false learning that may have occurred, make the students themselves aware of their thinking, and create sound frameworks. The idea is that formative assessments are entities that prepare the student's mind for thinking, not outcomes (Chappuis, 2009; Marzano, 2006).

What this means to proficiency-based teachers is that students need to constantly monitor their performance on formative assessments and learn from them—they must see any mismatch between what they expected to happen and what actually happened. Really, the responsibility the teacher has during the formative assessment process is to provide assessments that bring student thinking patterns to light and ensure that students identify them. But to pull this off, teachers need to have a mindset that embraces student-led reflective learning and to resist the urge to use formatives to *verify* learning.

One example where we see formative learning used *by* students instead of *for* students is by encouraging assessment graphing (Marzano, 2010). Assessment graphs are nothing new; however, in proficiency-based assessment, the teacher *must* manipulate the variables that the students use to graph. The particular example in figure 6.3 shows students comparing their preparation time and study of the content with the impact an error had on overall performance. Each dot represents a singular error on an assessment. Notice that the student in this example plotted the mistakes caused by low prep time as having a major effect on his or her performance.

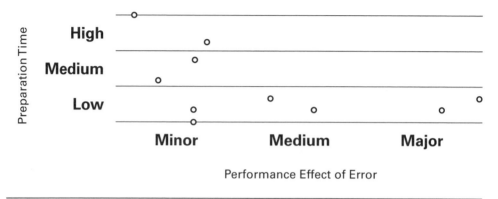

Figure 6.3: A student plotting preparation time versus performance effect of error.

In this example, this particular student saw the lower the prep time for the exam, the more major mistakes began to happen. Although minor errors occurred even with high prep time, the more this student did not value his or her formative practice, the more apt he or she was to make a major mistake. Notice that no major negative impact occurred with moderate or high engagement with the formative practice. The teacher and student alike can deduce that formative practice must be engaged in more purposefully. It may also mean in this case that the student is failing to react to his or her own errors during the formative process or even further still that the student is not accepting formative feedback. All of these are far more informative intervention steps than simply reviewing the content with the student.

Another example of this plotting exercise, shown in figure 6.4, includes a confidence ranking of each question. This particular student shows that when he or she felt more confident but erred, it actually had a major impact on performance.

If we now look at this graph from the reflective learner's eyes we can deduce that when the student erred on questions he or she was more confident on, this had a major negative impact on his or her overall performance. A teacher and student alike can take this to mean that the student has a fundamental misconception about a major principle or aspect of the content. Therefore they must review their portfolio of formatives to identify the area of the proficiency-based target that may be misunderstood.

Proficiency-based instruction challenges teachers to create *proficiency-based learning experiences* instead of *lessons*. These experiences demand that students make errors and be keen observers of their own thinking. In other words, to learn, students need to engage with material and observe themselves making mistakes. Through performances on formatives related to rigorous proficiency-based targets, students gain knowledge and grow in their competency when they are able to reflect on their errors. In other words, lessons must be dynamic and changing, pivoting on the thinking of the student as it relates to the errors, misconceptions, or faulty logic patterns they may possess (Marzano, 2006).

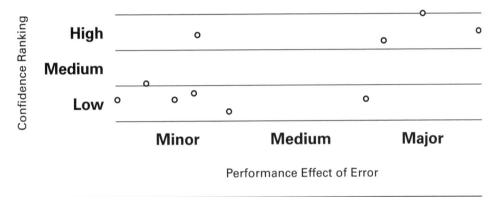

Figure 6.4: A student plotting confidence ranking versus performance effect of error.

Realization 3: Students Must Be Active Learners

We often tend to overestimate how much control students have over their own learning; in reality, we don't give them much. Therefore, students have a tendency to be passive participants in the learning process. We typically see teachers as responsible for the students' learning. If the teacher is responsible, then a student simply needs to pay attention, absorb, and then reproduce a model without really ever being active in the learning process. The reality is that students need a lot of practice setting goals, searching for the meaning of their thinking, and developing the skills to monitor their progress (Chappuis, 2009). Furthermore, students seldom look for evidence or feedback that disproves the fact that they are smart (Schoemaker, 2011). Students have a tendency to rationalize bad outcomes. In this way, they often distort feedback, and this suppresses learning (Schoemaker, 2011).

This idea made us wonder how the student is involved in learning. In his book *Brilliant Mistakes*, Schoemaker (2011) discusses how people have many pathways to choose from as they make a decision, but they tend to pick the pathways that rationalize away feedback and error because there is simply not enough evidence that allows the learner to separate learning from background noise. Schoemaker illustrates this through flowcharts he refers to as *learning loops*. As teachers nuance their understanding of proficiency-based assessment, they begin to realize that students are involved in similar loops.

When developing proficiency-based assessment, we set out to use Schoemaker's idea to uncover how active students are in the learning process. When we sat down and discussed our experiences both as teachers and administrators, we were able to plot a common path that learning was taking on a similar type of flowchart, shown in figure 6.5.

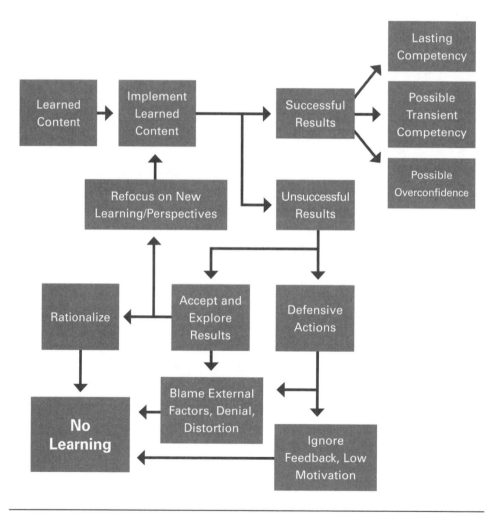

Figure 6.5: What traditional learning looks like.

As we stated in earlier chapters, learning is complex and dynamic, and this chart shows why. This demonstrates not only an outcomes-based model of learning but also how complicated learning actually is. Learners work hard to maintain the top level of this loop—the successful results path—and teachers work even harder to keep students out of the bottom loops, where rationalization and blame become the norm (Schoemaker, 2011).

Also, notice that there is no opportunity for students to explore their performance and assume *accountability* for it. Teachers shuttle students toward the successful results, in the top right corner of the chart. Teachers know that the bottom loops exist, and they avoid them at all costs for one reason: these loops feel like failure. Instead, we should hold the students accountable when they enter into these bottom loops and use those loops to encourage them to become excellent self-assessors of their performance.

After seeing that traditional outcomes-based flowchart, we decided to create one reflecting proficiency-based assessment (see figure 6.6), structured around the idea of a *search for and reaction to results* instead of trying to *achieve outcomes* (Chappuis, 2009)— an idea we have outlined in earlier chapters as a core principle of proficiency-based assessment.

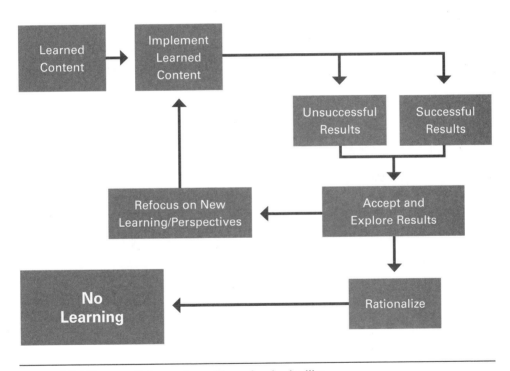

Figure 6.6: What proficiency-based learning looks like.

As we see in the bottom area of the flowchart, we can successfully hold all students accountable for reflection. All students must accept and explore results. There is no option to not do it. Thus the "no learning" outcome is reduced to one cause: a student rationalizing the results instead of exploring them. In this proficiency-based chart, rationalization is much more preventable than in the first outcomes-based chart.

In this loop, students are forced to become active, because active review and reflection is the only option after they implement learned content. Whether they are right or wrong, successful or unsuccessful, they must act and react. Since all students, whether right or wrong, must review their work, learning accountability shifts from the teacher to the student, and assessment shifts from outcomes to reflective refocusing. If all students become active thinkers and reflectors, learning becomes a journey of reflective insight, not a journey that strives to obtain outcomes. John Hattie (2012), in his book *Visible Learning for Teachers*, says it best: "The fundamental premise is that all students should be educated in ways that develop their capability to assess their own learning" (p. 141).

Realization 4: Teachers Must Avoid Feedback Distortion

Most students look for feedback that supports only their view of learning, and when they get feedback about a poor performance, students tend to justify that it was some external force that caused the wrong answer. In essence, learners have a strong tendency to suppress errors and obscure important lessons from feedback simply because they don't see it as an accurate representation of self (Schoemaker, 2011).

Students must trust feedback to accept it and to learn from it. Therefore, they need the *right* feedback that is digestible, actionable, and accepted. The right feedback encourages diversity of thought and outlines how to challenge thinking (Wiliam, 2011). This can be accomplished with feedback that is guided by a proficiency-based target. Proficiency-based feedback is the only way a student can make accurate sense of content presented in a dynamic and complex lesson. Proficiency-based assessment outlines several questions, derived from Schoemaker's (2011) work, for teachers to ask to ensure accurate feedback about student performance.

- **Is the feedback biased?** Do you have any preconceptions about the student work that may cause you to *assume* why a student got an answer right or got it wrong? Any preconceptions will cause the feedback to be unreliable.

- **Does the feedback have context?** Is your feedback based in a too-familiar context or in line with what students expect to focus on?

- **Are the students ready?** Does your lesson allow students to become prepared to receive the feedback?

- **What data do the feedback rely on?** Is your feedback reliant on the most readily available data or a full data set of student performance?

Feedback from a partial or incorrect data set can cause feedback to be untrustworthy.

- **Is the feedback clear?** Is the learning you want the students to grow from present in the feedback, or do you just have deficiency language?

- **Is the feedback balanced?** Does your feedback have both performance and learning quality?

- **Is the feedback relevant?** Does the feedback relate to the target? Does it contain the aspects of proficiency from the target?

By using these questions, teachers can increase the value of their feedback, thus increasing the rate of feedback acceptance (Ilgen, Fisher, & Taylor, 1979). But the most important question of all is, Are your students ready? When a target is proficiency-based and the students are ready to receive, react to, and accept feedback, that feedback becomes more valued and creates a rewarding learning experience.

Key Points

Following are key points from the chapter that readers should review to ensure they have a firm grasp on the content.

- The coming together of curriculum, instruction, and assessment should be clearer to the team members as they elaborate on their evaluation. These three elements should be more aligned and interlocked.

- The elaboration phase is directed toward bridging gaps in learning. The team should be identifying better strategies to provide students to bridge these gaps.

- Collaborative teams are in the business of continuous professional growth and continuous student growth. This mindset requires resiliency on the part of teachers and students. Elaboration reminds us to be flexible in our teaching and learning. There are many ways to approach instruction for the success of every student.

Epilogue

Professional Learning as a Creative Process

The focus of this book revolved around proficiency-based assessment. While there are many topics within education that can be explored using this professional learning framework, we decided to begin with this educational idea because we think shifting the way we approach assessment will help U.S. schooling move in a better, more thoughtful, and more sophisticated direction—beyond what are now antiquated approaches to assessment that don't provide the needed, articulated clarity learners need to participate in their own growth and capacity building.

Professional learning is a creative process. As you have finished reading about our team's journey through the change process, we want to reassert the most significant characteristic of these teachers' collaboration toward change: it was never easy or streamlined. Preparation overlapped with incubation and evaluation. Evaluation required going back to preparation and insight. The journey is not a straight road to change. It is very often recursive; it doubles back, overlaps, and often takes two steps forward and one step back. It is highly reflective and raises many questions. Likewise, as we saw, different teammates are often at different points in the creative process. These variables challenge leaders to balance the overlapping understandings, perspectives, and capacities for change. While challenging, when all of these variables are circulating, better decisions about learning develop because smarter checks and balances are in place. More significantly, continuous improvement sustains.

During our work with teams that function through a creative process, ongoing revisions take place. We often observe teams begin to interact swiftly from evaluation to elaboration to insight. The process becomes self-perpetuating, and through collaboration, more and more students benefit from this constantly circulating dialogue around learning. Teams begin to more fully educate themselves about the changes they are making, and they constantly collaborate over ideas, build on each other's good thinking, and make learning gains for student growth.

As teammates continue to support each other to think differently and to continuously develop ideas about better instructional efforts to reach students, remember to constantly give back to the profession at large. It is essential that we are building off each other's creative-thinking processes, gaining multiple insights around reaching all students, and collaborating over what we are doing to bridge gaps in learning.

The conversations regarding learning targets, proficiency, and feedback are highly demanding, but anything worthwhile is. Paying thoughtful attention and providing better leadership to teams of teachers can help to really create and build these changes in a way that will be positive for school culture and ensure that student learning thrives. But the commitment to proficiency-based assessment cannot end here. As educators, we must make a commitment to examining our grading and assessment practices so they align to this strong approach to teaching and learning. We must open a greater, more reflective dialogue with our students around the standards of work we expect of them and the evidence of learning we want students to produce.

References and Resources

Ainsworth, L., & Viegut, D. (2006). *Common formative assessments: How to connect standards-based instruction and assessment.* Thousand Oaks, CA: Corwin Press.

Amabile, T. M. (1983). *The social psychology of creativity.* New York: Springer-Verlag.

Badders, W. (2000). *Methods of assessment.* Accessed at www.eduplace.com/science /profdev/articles/badders.html on June 29, 2013.

Bailey, K., & Jakicic, C. (2012). *Common formative assessment: A toolkit for Professional Learning Communities at Work.* Bloomington, IN: Solution Tree Press.

Bell, S. T., & Arthur, W., Jr. (2008). Feedback acceptance in developmental assessment centers: The role of feedback message, participant personality, and affective response to the feedback session. *Journal of Organizational Behavior, 29*(5), 681–703.

Black, P., & Wiliam, D. (1998). Inside the black box: Raising standards through classroom assessment. *Phi Delta Kappan, 80*(2), 139–148.

Chappuis, J. (2009). *Seven strategies of assessment for learning.* Portland, OR: Educational Testing Service.

Chappuis, S., & Chappuis, J. (2007–2008). The best value in formative assessment. *Educational Leadership, 65*(4), 14–19.

Chappuis, S., & Stiggins, R. J. (2002). Classroom assessment for learning. *Educational Leadership, 60*(1), 40–43.

Coutu, D. L. (2002). How resilience works. *Harvard Business Review, 80*(5), 46–50, 52, 55.

Csikszentmihalyi, M. (1990). *Flow: The psychology of optimal experience.* New York: Harper & Row.

Danielson, C. (2007). *Enhancing professional practice: A framework for teaching* (2nd ed.). Alexandria, VA: Association for Supervision and Curriculum Development.

Danielson, C. (2011). *The framework for teaching: Evaluation instrument.* Princeton, NJ: The Danielson Group.

DuFour, R., DuFour, R., Eaker, R., & Karhanek, G. (2004). *Whatever it takes: How professional learning communities respond when kids don't learn.* Bloomington, IN: Solution Tree Press.

DuFour, R., DuFour, R., Eaker, R., & Karhanek, G. (2010). *Raising the bar and closing the gap: Whatever it takes.* Bloomington, IN: Solution Tree Press.

Elbaum, D., & Reibel, A. (2015). A.C.T. Explorer Reading Model: Combining formative assessment and reading strategies. *The Assessor, 3*(3).

Guskey, T. R., & Jung, L. A. (2013). *Answers to essential questions about standards, assessments, grading, and reporting.* Thousand Oaks, CA: Corwin Press.

Hattie, J. (2012). *Visible learning for teachers: Maximizing impact on learning.* London: Routledge.

Ilgen, D., Fisher, C., & Taylor, M. (1979). Consequences of individual feedback on behavior in organizations. *Journal of Applied Psychology, 64*(4), 349–371.

JayMJ23. (n.d.). *Michael Jordan "Failure" Nike commercial* [Video file]. Accessed at www.youtube.com/watch?v=45mMioJ5szc&feature=youtu.be on April 22, 2015.

Martin-Kniep, G. O. (2000). *Becoming a better teacher: Eight innovations that work.* Alexandria, VA: Association for Supervision and Curriculum Development.

Marzano, R. J. (2003). *What works in schools: Translating research into action.* Alexandria, VA: Association for Supervision and Curriculum Development.

Marzano, R. J. (2006). *Classroom assessment & grading that work.* Alexandria, VA: Association for Supervision and Curriculum Development.

Marzano, R. J. (2007). *The art and science of teaching: A comprehensive framework for effective instruction.* Alexandria, VA: Association for Supervision and Curriculum Development.

Marzano, R. J. (2009). *Designing & teaching learning goals & objectives.* Bloomington, IN: Marzano Research.

Marzano, R. J. (2010). *Formative assessment and standards-based grading.* Bloomington, IN: Marzano Research.

Marzano, R. J., & Pickering, D. J. (2011). *The highly engaged classroom.* Bloomington, IN: Marzano Research.

Millhiser, W. (2010, January 8). *Plus/minus grading systems* [Web log post]. Accessed at http://blsciblogs.baruch.cuny.edu/teachingblog/2010/01/08/plusminus-grading-systems on December 17, 2014.

Moss, C. M., & Brookhart, S. M. (2012). *Learning targets: Helping students aim for understanding in today's lesson.* Alexandria, VA: Association for Supervision and Curriculum Development.

Moss, C. M., Brookhart, S. M., & Long, B. A. (2011). Know your learning target. *Educational Leadership, 68*(6), 66–69.

National Governors Association Center for Best Practices & Council of Chief State School Officers. (2010). *Common Core State Standards for English language arts and literacy in history/social studies, science, and technical subjects.* Washington, DC: Authors. Accessed at www.corestandards.org/assets/CCSSI_ELA%20Standards.pdf on August 10, 2015.

Popham, W. (2008). *Transformative assessment*. Alexandria, VA: Association for Supervision and Curriculum Development.

Popham, W. (2009). *Instruction that measures up: Successful teaching in the age of accountability*. Alexandria, VA: Association for Supervision and Curriculum Development.

Ripley, A. (2013). *The smartest kids in the world: And how they got that way*. New York: Simon & Schuster.

Ritchhart, R., Church, M., & Morrison, K. (2011). *Making thinking visible: How to promote engagement, understanding, and independence for all learners*. San Francisco: Jossey-Bass.

Sandrock, P. (2011, December 8). *Designing backwards: From performance assessments to units of instruction*. Lecture presented at the American Council on the Teaching of Foreign Languages, Lincolnshire, IL.

Schoemaker, P. J. H. (2011). *Brilliant mistakes: Finding success on the far side of failure* [E-reader version]. Philadelphia: Wharton Digital Press.

Schwartz, T., & McCarthy, C. (2007). Manage your energy, not your time. *Harvard Business Review, 85*, 63–73.

Sinek, S. (2009). *Start with why: How great leaders inspire everyone to take action*. New York: Portfolio.

Stiggins, R. J. (2001a). *Student-involved classroom assessment* (3rd ed.). Upper Saddle River, NJ: Merrill Prentice Hall.

Stiggins, R. J. (2001b). The unfulfilled promise of classroom assessment. *Educational Measurement: Issues and Practice, 20*(3), 5–15.

Stiggins, R. J. (2007). Assessment through the student's eyes. *Educational Leadership, 64*(8), 22–26.

Stiggins, R. J. (2008). *Assessment manifesto: A call for the development of balance assessment systems* [Position paper]. Portland, OR: ETS Assessment Training Institute.

Stiggins, R. J., Arter, J. A., Chappuis, J., & Chappuis, S. (2004). *Classroom assessment for student learning: Doing it right—Using it well*. Portland, OR: Assessment Training Institute.

Stiggins, R. J., Arter, J. A., Chappuis, J., & Chappuis, S. (2012). *Classroom assessment for student learning: Doing it right—Using it well* (2nd ed.). Portland, OR: Assessment Training Institute.

Stiggins, R. J., & Chappuis, J. (2005). Using student-involved classroom assessment to close achievement gaps. *Theory Into Practice, 44*(1), 11–18.

Stiggins, R. J., & Chappuis, J. (2008). Enhancing student learning. *District Administration, 44*(1), 42–44.

Stiggins, R. J., & Chappuis, J. (2012). *An introduction to student-involved assessment for learning* (6th ed.). Boston: Pearson.

Tough, P. (2012). *How children succeed: Grit, curiosity, and the hidden power of character.* New York: Houghton Mifflin Harcourt.

Valli, L. (1997). Listening to other voices: A description of teacher reflection in the United States. *Peabody Journal of Education, 72*(1), 67–88.

Wiggins, G., & McTighe, J. (2005). *Understanding by design* (Expanded 2nd ed.). Alexandria, VA: Association for Supervision and Curriculum Development.

Wiliam, D. (2011). *Embedded formative assessment.* Bloomington, IN: Solution Tree Press.

Wormeli, R. (2013). *The collected writings (so far) of Rick Wormeli: Crazy good stuff I've learned about teaching along the way* [E-reader version]. Westerville, OH: Association for Middle Level Education.

Wormeli, R. (2014). Perseverance and grit. *AMLE Magazine, 1*(5), 41–43.

Index

On Your Mark
By Thomas R. Guskey
Create and sustain a learning environment where students thrive and stakeholders are accurately informed of student progress. Clarify the purpose of grades, craft a vision statement aligned with this purpose, and discover research-based strategies to implement effective grading and reporting practices.
BKF606

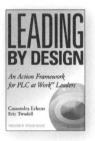

Leading by Design
By Cassandra Erkens and Eric Twadell
Foreword by Richard DuFour
After interviewing and observing principals, administrators, and teachers, the authors identify seven leadership practices that effective PLC leaders share, along with the techniques that have led them to sustainable success.
BKF430

Design in Five
By Nicole Dimich Vagle
Foreword by Douglas Reeves
Discover how to work with your school team to create innovative, effective, engaging assessments using a five-phase design protocol. Explore various types of assessment, learn the traits of quality assessment, and evaluate whether your current assessments meet the design criteria.
BKF604

The Assessment Toolkit
Transform your assessment practice into a powerful tool that inspires student learning. Find tips on how to involve students in the assessment process, integrate assessments into instruction, and help your team begin to build its own repertoire of assessments.
KTF132

a division of

Solution Tree | Press
Solution Tree

Visit solution-tree.com or call 800.733.6786 to order.